Religion and Morality

Religion and Morality

An Introduction

Paul W. Diener

Westminster John Knox Press
Louisville, Kentucky

Scripture quotations from the New Revised Standard Version
of the Bible are copyright © 1989 by the Division of Christian Education
of the National Council of the Churches of Christ in the U.S.A.
and are used by permission.

Book and cover design by Jennifer K. Cox
Cover image © 1997 PhotoDisc, Inc.

First Edition
Published by Westminster John Knox Press
Louisville, Kentucky

This book is printed on acid-free paper that meets the
American National Standards Institute Z39.48 standard. ♾

PRINTED IN THE UNITED STATES OF AMERICA
96 97 98 99 00 01 02 03 04 05 — 10 9 8 7 6 5 4 3 2 1

Library of Congress Cataloging-in-Publication Data

Diener, Paul W., date.
 Religion and morality : an introduction / Paul W. Diener. — 1st ed.
  p.   cm.
 Includes bibliographical references and index.
 ISBN 0-664-25765-8 (alk. paper)
 1. Religion and ethics.   I. Title.
BJ47.D54   1997
291.5—dc21   97-14698

*Dedicated with affection to
Shirley, partner for almost fifty years,
and to our five children—
Bill, Tim, Becky, Mark, and Lisa*

Contents

Preface

Many people have helped to make this work possible. At the risk of overlooking some, I wish to mention several persons who provided valuable assistance.

I am grateful to York College of Pennsylvania for the provision of a sabbatical and reduced teaching load for several semesters, which enabled me to work on this project. The academic dean, Dr. William A. DeMeester, and our department chair, Dr. Edward Jones, were most cooperative in this regard.

The Society of Christian Philosophers deserves thanks also, for they allowed me to read a paper on this subject, which was subsequently expanded to the present work.

Four colleagues in York College of Pennsylvania deserve special recognition for reading this manuscript and making very constructive suggestions for improvement: Dr. Melvin Kulbicki, Dr. Edward Jones, Dr. Dennis Weiss, and adjunct professor Richard Cleary.

Two friends also helped: Mr. Gerry Marple read this work with enthusiasm and helped me to clarify several points. The Rev. Donald Repsher, an old friend who is well versed in environmental matters, came forth with great ideas for improving chapter 7.

The secretary of York College's department of education, Ms. Susan Savia, furnished word processing and proofreading skills, which greatly helped to get the manuscript ready for the publisher.

I am also indebted to Timothy Staveteig and Jon Berquist, editors at Westminster John Knox, who offered encouragement and pertinent advice.

Last, and most importantly, I am grateful to my wife, Shirley, who, beyond the good advice she gave about my writing style, has always supported me and the vocation I have followed. To her, and our children, I lovingly dedicate this work.

Introduction

Religion and morality: Are they connected, related? Should they be friends, foes, or forbearers of each other? I wish to argue that they should be good friends—the kinds of friends who respect each other's freedom and autonomy.

In pursuing this argument, I begin by describing religion as a human activity (chapter 1), followed by descriptions of morality from both a religious and a philosophical or secular perspective (chapters 2 and 3). Chapters 4 through 6 go to the heart of the matter through a critical exploration of the three possible ways for religion and morality to confront and encounter each other:

1. They may be so close as to be virtually *inseparable.*
2. They may be two completely distinct and different activities and therefore entirely *separable.*
3. They may be neither altogether inseparable nor entirely separable, but *relational.*

In this work I will try to show all three options as viable and defensible.

The religious approach to morality tends to take the first option, while a secular approach generally favors the second option. The alternative of the third approach encourages taking the best of the two apparently contradictory options. This alternative attempts to bridge the gap between an exclusively religious and an exclusively secular approach.

The concluding chapter represents an attempt to apply the *relational* approach to a specific moral issue within environmental ethics, that of preserving species. The purpose is that of showing how a relational approach, a dialogue between religious and philosophical ethics, is fruitful and constructive.

Chapter 1

What Is Religion?

Before describing the relationship of religion and morality, the nature of religion and morality must be discussed. What is religion? What is morality? Despite their common use, these words are frustratingly difficult to satisfactorily define. So let me try to describe these words.

In contrast to morality, the origin of the word *religion* is etymologically debatable. The root word could be the Latin word *religio* (meaning obligation or bond) or the Latin word *religare* (meaning to tie or bind). Religion scholars seem to prefer *religare*. Etymological uncertainty about this word contributes to the abundance of definitions of religion. Within these definitions common elements are found, but it is obvious that no one definition of religion prevails.

An Elusive Subject

There are several reasons why the word religion is difficult to describe. One reason is that people usually perceive things from their own perspective. The stance of the observer and participant applies to the way people regard religion, as well as morality, politics, and art. No two people see an activity exactly the same way. As unique selves, people look at things according to personality, temperament, and background. Eastern and Western peoples see the world differently. What we see depends on where we stand or sit. The stance of the observer is crucial.

It is possible to see the activity of religion from various vantage points: from within only, from half-within, from half-without, from fully detached, and from detached within. Actually, fully detached may be impossible, for it is doubtful that observers or participants can remove themselves from the place where they stand. The highly prized value of complete objectivity may be unachievable.

In describing religion it is very easy to be one-sided. We tend to highlight what is most appealing, attractive, and important—to us! Religion as an activity has many sides: institutional, devotional, doctrinal, mystical, static, ecstatic, substantive, functional, exoteric, and esoteric.[1]

The strong feelings people have about religion as a human activity also come into play. Some humans are very fond of religion and what it involves; others passionately dislike what it represents. Still others neither like nor dislike, but are merely indifferent. Our age has witnessed strong personal antipathies to religion from several quarters. Social scientists like Freud and Marx attacked religion vehemently. Philosophers like Nietzsche and Feuerbach made biting comments against it. An American novelist, Walker Percy, declares the word religion to be moribund, smelling of dust and wax. And a recent theologian, Karl Barth, has thundered that "God hates religion," viewing religion as something humans create to make God conform to their own desires. Others have pointed out that the word religion is not found in the Jewish Bible and only four times in the Christian Bible. Many of the people I meet prefer the word spirituality to the word religion. Those of us who still use the word religion often find ourselves on the defensive.

Contemporary Western thinkers sympathetic to religion tend to favor the mystical/devotional side of religion to the exclusion of the other sides. Since the European Enlightenment, Western intellectuals have seen religion as primarily a private, individual affair. They regard religion in a Whiteheadian way, as what "one does with his solitariness." Contemporary society contains a good number of "cultured despisers" of religion, who become especially critical when religion shows its public and social dimension and takes positions on issues like war, abortion, the environment, and the economy. As these critics see it, religion should keep out of the political arena and stay in the private realm.

Another factor contributing to the complexity of describing religion can be traced to the academic situation. Religion is studied carefully by scholars from diverse academic disciplines. Historians study the history of religion, psychologists the psychology and phenomenology of religion. Sociologists and anthropologists study religion with the methods of their discipline. Philosophers delve into the underlying assumptions of religion. And religion scholars engage in "comparative religion"—looking for the similarities and differences of religious traditions. Naturally, religion will be described differently by persons working in different disciplines; a sociologist will not describe religion the way a historian or philosopher would. Because of diverse approaches to religion, the likelihood of a common description eludes our grasp.

Religion is not easily described because of its variety and diversity. The ways of "doing" or practicing religion may be uncountable. Religion is not just one thing; it is a many-sided, "many-splendored" thing. Religious communities are manifold and exceedingly diverse. Ninian Smart handles this variety well by focusing on the six dimensions of religion: experiential, mythical, doctrinal, ethical, ritual, and social. *Experiential* refers to religious experience, being confronted by the numinous (the holy, sacred, transcendent), or attaining a mystical state of union with ultimate reality. The *mythical* dimension pertains to stories of great symbolic depth that help answer the ultimate questions of life and death. The *doctrinal* dimension is the formal, systematized teachings of a given religious tradition (e.g., the Trinity in Christianity, nirvana in Buddhism). The *ethical* dimension deals with how people within a particular religion should behave, or how an ideal human being should live. The dimension of *ritual* relates to ways in which myths, doctrines, and moral values are acted out, often through sacrificial and/or initiatory rites (e.g., prayers, offerings, sacraments, rites of passage). The social dimension has to do with the ways in which religions organize and situate themselves in the larger society—the institutional side.[2] No matter how well chosen they may be, an activity including these dimensions cannot be described in a few words.

Furthermore, members of one particular religion often practice it very differently. Each religious tradition has those who strongly believe that the originating experiences, stories, and doctrines should be kept literally and completely—the orthodox, conservatives, or fundamentalists of a religion. Each religion also has those who are willing to deviate, depart, and develop, or engage in what Pope John XXIII called *aggiornamento* (bringing up to date)—the liberals, progressives, and modernists. Unfortunately, descriptive words become labels and even smear words, and in the process lose their usefulness.

Another indication of the diversity of religion is reflected in the fluid ways in which groups or persons refer to themselves, or are referred to, as religious. The American Humanist Association, for example, as a consistent critic of traditional religion, refers to humanism in its *Humanist Manifesto I & II* as the highest expression of religious faith. Similarly, sociologists and theologians allude to Marxism/Communism as a religion or quasi-religion. A word that is used to refer to activities or ideas often seen as both religious and antireligious in nature is rather slippery. Attempts to find other words are understandable.

A particularly dramatic way in which religions vary greatly is in the ways they view God or ultimate reality. The three great Western religions—Judaism, Christianity, and Islam—view God as a personal being to be revered and obeyed. The God of these religions is described as omnipotent, omniscient, and omnipresent—the theistic point of view.

In the Eastern religions of Hinduism, Buddhism, and Taoism, however, ultimate reality is usually seen in a nonpersonal way. Buddhists assert that they do not believe in a personal God. This means that by some traditional definitions of religion (e.g., belief in God or a supreme being) Buddhism,

Taoism, and possibly Hinduism would not qualify as religions. The very different ways in which religions view ultimate reality explains the preference of many scholars for broader, more inclusive descriptions of religion.

As a human activity, religion is dynamic rather than static. Religions exist within cultures that grow and change. Fritjof Capra, a scientist, and theologian David Steindl-Rast talk about "new paradigms" in science and theology. Any activity that develops and evolves is hard to pin down, define, or adequately describe.

Lastly, religion is difficult to describe because estimations of its strengths and weakness vary greatly. Some argue that religions are declining; sociologists of religion contend that secularization is winning, especially in affluent nations. Cited as evidence of decline is the fact that in the United States membership and attendance in mainline churches and synagogues has fallen. A major newsmagazine (*Newsweek*, Dec. 7, 1992) has declared that the so-called Judeo-Christian tradition no longer exists in modern pluralist America.

However, the evidence is mixed: the Christian religion may be declining in Europe and North America, but it is expanding in some areas of Africa and Asia. Furthermore, the religions of Hinduism, Buddhism, Taoism, Confucianism, and Shintoism exhibit continuing vitality in their geographical areas. And although the mainline branches of Judaism and Christianity are struggling to remain vital in the United States, some of the more conservative wings of these religious groups are thriving. Also, in the United States, the emergence of "New Age" religion or spirituality indicates that religion in its diverse dimensions is not yet dead or dying. The fact that conflict between religions has intensified in some areas of the world points to vitality; dead people don't fight! Mark Juergensmeyer actually says that religious conflict is the new Cold War. The situation described here helps us understand why religion is not easily described.

A Whole Greater than Its Parts

Despite the problems in describing religion, the question posed for this chapter remains: What is religion? Definitions and descriptions may be unsatisfactory, but several words and ideas keep appearing when religion is discussed. I wish to highlight seven of these ideas and point to them as integral *parts* of the remarkable *whole* we are calling religion.

Inner Attitudes

Religion is connected with inner attitudes involving such human acts as believing, trusting, depending, and faithing (to verbalize a noun that is really an action). It also pertains to attitudes related to confidence, courage, and hope, very close to what Carl Jung once declared the greatest need of his patients for them to fully recover, namely, a "religious outlook."

Among the written descriptions of religion that fit this particular aspect are the following: beliefs about what is ultimately important, a rational trust in reality, "immortal longings," living by convictions that make life ultimately worth living, what we trust as giving meaning and value to our lives, an attitude toward what is considered a determiner of destiny, a dependence on powers believed to control and direct the course of nature and life, a feeling of ultimate dependence on the Ultimate, a feeling of something "unlimited and unbounded," a belief in the ultimate meaning of the universe, convictions about the context and purpose of human life as such, "a divine light in the life of the soul," a surrender to the will of God in all things, beliefs that help to give hope, courage, and confidence, and the binding stance one takes toward the mystery of life and death.[3]

Seeking Answers and Meaning

Religion is also connected with the compelling human tendency to find answers for ultimate questions, to discover the meaning of life and death. A Jewish Holocaust survivor, Dr. Viktor Frankl, in a popular book titled *Man's Search for Meaning*, contends that people can endure suffering if they find meaning in it. Making religion a search for meaning is general and broad, but searching for answers and meaning is one part of the total phenomenon called religion.

Descriptions that illustrate this part of religion are: exploration of the ultimate meaning of life, involvement in the meaning of existence and finding our relation to the significant events of life, holistic interpretations of life that enable us to make sense of emotions, desires, and attitudes, and thinking on the ultimate questions of life, death, and reality.[4]

Three significant ultimate questions humans ask as they seek the meaning of life are those of origin, destiny, and meaning: Where did I come from? Where will I end (my final destiny)? What is the purpose of the life I now live? When persons sincerely ask these questions they participate in one of the salient parts of religion.

Encounter with Ultimate Reality

Religion also has much to do with the human desire for contact with ultimate reality, which is also called the Transcendent, the Sacred, the Supreme Being, the Powers/Forces of the Universe, or God. One's picture or understanding of reality conveyed in these words constitutes a "worldview." The fact that humans adopt worldviews has been emphasized recently. Walter Wink succinctly characterizes five basic worldviews:

1. The Ancient Worldview, which is biblical but not uniquely biblical, is one in which everything earthly has a heavenly counterpart and vice versa. If there is war on earth, there is war in heaven; events occurring in heaven are mirrored on earth. Most ancient peoples had this worldview.

2. The Spiritualistic Worldview divides humans into soul and body. Matter and creation are evil. The soul is trapped in a body until it finds its way back to heaven, from whence it came. This view is strong in Platonism and gnosticism.

3. The Materialistic Worldview has no heaven, God, or soul, but only a material existence, which is known through the five senses. At death humans cease to exist except as chemicals and atoms that once constituted them.

4. The Theological Worldview posits a supernatural realm not known by the senses, and an earthly realm known by science but isolated from the supernatural.

5. An Integral Worldview sees everything as having an outer and an inner aspect. It is the spiritual aspect of the ancient or biblical worldview that affirms an "interiority" in all things. It sees inner spiritual reality as closely related to an outer physical representation.[5]

Among descriptions of religion that embrace a combination of the ancient, biblical, and integral worldviews are: a conception of the general order of existence, an unseen order in which our supreme good lies in adjusting ourselves to it, the self-transcendence toward what is ultimate and unconditional in meaning, an experience in which metahuman reality is injected into human life, participation in something of intrinsic meaning, attributing a sacredness to the world and nature, a basic attitude arising in an encounter with the whole of reality given to one in one's existence, a sense of the sacred, sense of a "benign empowering reality," and a relation with something thought to be of life-shaping importance.[6]

This part of religion highlights the transcendent, that which is higher than and beyond us as human beings but known and apprehended in the inner and deepest self. It remains one of the essential parts of religion.

Desire for Relationship and Experience

Religion also has to do with the human desire for a relationship with and an experience of ultimate reality, the transcendent, and the sacred. This part of religion naturally grows out of an emphasis on a higher reality than ourselves which can be known. This experiential dimension speaks of things like religious experience, mysticism, a heightened consciousness, a spiritual birth, and so forth. It also pertains to the ritual dimension, which centers on activities that enhance relationship and experience, such as prayer and meditation.

Among descriptions of religion that highlight this part are: the relation between God and human beings, aligning believers with a transcendent reality, symbols that establish moods and motivation, making connection to something larger, attempting to establish a right relation between ourselves and something outside ourselves, and an energy-releasing event that raises life to higher power.[7] The experiential dimension of religion continues to fascinate despite the increasing secularization of modern life.

An Act of Valuing

Religion is also related to the act of valuing, evaluating what is of superior or supreme worth and truly good. Religion is a way of valuing. This part of religion is highlighted by the English novelist/philosopher Iris Murdoch, who is fond of Plato's insistence on seeking the idea or form of the Good. For Murdoch, religion is primarily "a mode of belief in the sovereign place of goodness and virtue in human life."[8] Murdoch does not use the word value, but her view of religion as a pursuit of what is truly good places her among those who focus on religion as an act of valuing.

Other descriptions of this part of religion are: an expression of human evaluation and ultimate loyalties, whatever is regarded as ultimate in being and value, that which determines life and destiny and is thought to be of importance in the nature of things, that which offers us vision and values, concern about experiences that are regarded to be of supreme value, and activity pursued in behalf of an ideal and against obstacles in spite of threats of personal loss because of the conviction of its general and enduring value.[9] In a society in which one often hears such phrases as "family values" and "a crisis in values," the part of religion that emphasizes valuing should have relevance.

A Yearning for Self-Transformation

As a human activity, religion also has to do with the human desire for self-transformation, salvation, liberation, and becoming more human. Becoming a better person and demonstrating this by behavior, quality of life, or morality has been a prominent part of religion. Religions are eager to show people how they can be changed, liberated, and reborn. Religions presuppose that people can become better and different from what they were before the transformation began.

Among descriptions of religion that center on this aspect are: seeking to align believers with a transforming reality in order to achieve liberation or salvation, living according to the transcendent reality one encounters, a way to be human, living in wholehearted devotion to absolute goodness, that which provides strength and courage, "the perception of the infinite under such manifestations as are able to influence the moral character of man," a system of general truths which have the effect of transforming character when they are sincerely held and vividly apprehended, and a quest for self-transformation.[10]

This particular part of religion comes very close to morality, and explains why some people tend to conflate religion and morality. Wolfhart Pannenberg has noted that after Kant many German theologians saw religion as a product of moral consciousness, and in so doing neglected the experiential and mythical dimensions of religion.[11] Nevertheless, the desire to be a better person will continue to be an important part of religion.

The Need for Community

Religion also has a bearing on the human need for communities that support and encourage persons in the parts of religion previously noted. This can be designated as the social side of religion, just as important as the personal and inner side.

A respected American sociologist, Robert Bellah, along with colleagues has pursued the need of people to belong, to be part of communities that nourish and enrich their lives. In *Habits of the Heart*, Bellah argued that many Americans, because of their pursuit of "rugged individualism," have failed to find the communities they need. People live richer and fuller lives when they become part of meaningful communities.

In *The Courage to Be*, Paul Tillich showed that the courage to be a self and the courage to be a part of a community are necessary for human well-being. Rabbi Harold Kushner is correct in affirming that in communities "we learn to understand the world and grow to be human."[12]

Religion is not only concerned about relationships with ultimate reality; relationships with other humans are equally desirable.

With this description of the seven parts of religion, we have a starting point for our discussion. There could well be other parts. Are any of these parts more important than others? My response, from Gestalt psychology, is that "the whole is greater than the sum of its parts." Religion as a whole is what matters. The parts of religion are somewhat like the parts of that famous elephant in a popular poem, in which six blind men dogmatically proclaim just what an elephant is, based on the part they have touched! Touching all the parts of this many-splendored thing called religion seems preferable.

Nevertheless, because we are focusing on the relationship of religion and morality, we can ask which of the seven parts of religion are most connected with what is called morality. It seems obvious that religion as an act of valuing, a search for community, and a yearning for self-transformation has connections with morality. However, before drawing firm conclusions, we must investigate the activity called morality, which can be looked at from the perspective of religion as well as the perspective of philosophy. The next two chapters pursue this large topic.

Chapter 2

What Is Morality
(from a Religious Perspective)?

The word morality is no less difficult to define than the word religion, despite its prevalence as a human activity. Practicing morality and being a moral person go along with what it means to be human.

The word ethics is often used in association with morality, and the words are even commonly used interchangeably. We hear about people who are moral, as well as of people who are ethical. Prudence thus suggests that we consider these words together, as a package.

In contrast to the word religion, however, there is agreement on the origin of these words. According to the *Oxford English Dictionary (OED)*, the word ethics comes from the Greek word *ethos,* which primarily refers to character and/or manners. It is further defined as relating to morals, well-doing and not well-knowing only. Ethics is also said to pertain to the science of morals, a scheme of moral science, or a department of study concerned with the principles of human duty. Aristotle's writings on ethics are described as a treatise on the science of ethics, which leads to the further description of ethics as the moral principles or system of a particular thinker or school of thought. In the widest sense, therefore, ethics is the whole field of moral science, including the science of law.

The word morality is from the Latin *mores,* which also means manner or character. The various definitions of morality are very close to those just given for ethics. However, the *OED* also speaks of "moral" as pertaining to character and concerned with virtue and rules of right conduct. It further mentions the morals of a person or a community, or the habits and conduct of a person.

This brief etymological excursion shows two things: First, the words morality and ethics, from Greek and Latin words, are very close semantically. Their similarity in meaning justifies their interchangeable use. Second, a slight distinction between the two words is possible, in that morality seems to focus on human actions and practices, whereas ethics is primarily concerned with study and reflection on morality. Thus, when we refer to the morals or morality of a person, we are talking about their actual behavior. But when we speak of the ethics of a person we may be alluding to their written or unwritten reflections and thoughts about the nature of morality. In a word, morality is active and ethics is reflective, to the point of being philosophical and academic. Ethics is the subject taught in colleges and universities, although formerly it was called moral philosophy.

The starting point of morality and ethics is, therefore, very similar to that taken in religion: morality is an activity people engage in naturally and continually. Every day humans make judgments and decisions about how they should live and what they should do. On a daily basis we judge actions to be good or evil, right or wrong. Almost daily we are offended and horrified by events we read about or see on TV, on film, and in the real world. Gilbert Keith Chesterton wisely perceived that all denunciation has a moral basis.

Furthermore, our moral judgments and decisions are made in two major ways: religiously and/or philosophically. There is a religious morality—moral conduct that springs from religious beliefs and experiences. There is also a philosophical or secular morality—moral conduct that springs from philosophical beliefs and views. A religious and a philosophical or secular ethics are identifiable and describable. In this chapter I will discuss religious morality/ethics, and in the next chapter, philosophical or secular ethics. In pursuing this approach the great diversity within both religious and philosophical ethics will become evident.

Religious Morality/Ethics

Historically speaking, religious ethics may precede philosophical ethics. Peter Singer, an Australian philosopher, has edited a book entitled *A Companion to Ethics,* in which the great ethical traditions of the world's religions are discussed prior to the treatment of Western philosophical ethics. Singer acknowledges that the ethical traditions of the world's religious bodies are for most of the world's people "the living ethical systems to which they look for guidance."[1]

The influence of Judaism and Christianity on Western philosophy is generally accepted. If Western philosophical ethics begins with Socrates (470–399 B.C.E.), as most moral philosophers acknowledge, then the historical priority of Moses (13th century B.C.E.) and the Jewish prophets (8th century B.C.E. and following) are apparent.

The major living world religions include three Western religions—Judaism, Christianity, and Islam, and four Eastern religions—Hinduism, Buddhism, Confucianism, and Taoism. These religions have a significant numerical strength. A 1994 almanac showed that Judaism had almost 18 million members, Christianity had roughly 1.8 billion members, Islam had almost 1 billion members, Hinduism had almost 733 million adherents, Buddhism about 315 million, and Confucianism about 6 million or more members. No figures were given for Taoism, another Chinese religion. Shintoism, a religion largely confined to Japan, had over 3 million members. The total membership of the above religions, along with primitive/animistic religions, came to approximately 65 percent of the world's population.[2] If it is true that all religions have an ethical dimension, then the moral force of the world's living religions is indeed substantial. To a considerable extent, the people affiliated with these religions, however loosely, are influenced and guided by the moral ideals that these religions espouse and seek to apply.

Looking at the heart or essence of each particular religion prepares us for looking at religious ethics. In this attempt I am guided by John Hick's view of religion as "a culturally-conditioned response to an ultimate, transcendental reality."[3] The question as to whether these religions are the fruit of a divine revelation is avoided here, for it seems clear that even if revelation is present within a religion, the responses to revelation are at least partially influenced by cultural factors. With these thoughts in mind, I offer below my view of the essence of the world's religions.

Judaism

The Jewish religion begins with a man named Abraham, who lived originally in what is now Iraq, and in response to God's call migrated to present-day Israel, sometime between 2000 and 1750 B.C.E. Among his descendants was Moses, who delivered to the Jewish people a body of laws—the Ten Commandments and others—which helped to define them as a people. Between the eighth and fifth centuries B.C.E. a series of prophets preached and interpreted these laws, and later Jewish rabbis compiled a series of explanations and additional interpretations of these laws. Jews have envisioned God, whom they called Yahweh, Elohim, and Adonai, as holy and transcendent, one to be loved and greatly respected (or feared). This religion includes many stories about the Jewish people, the most important being the stories of an exodus from Egypt, the making of a covenant at Mount Sinai, and an exile in Babylonia (modern Iraq). Jewish theologians claim that the doctrinal dimension of Judaism is not great, but this religion contains definite beliefs about God—as Creator, as One, as Just, as One who calls, and so forth. Its morality/ethics spring largely from its understanding of God as holy, just, and merciful. This understanding affects the Jews' relationship with God and with other human beings. Such rituals as the Sabbath, along with Passover, Hanukkah, Yom Kippur, and other religious festivals, assist Jews in living a holy life, one dedicated to God. The Jewish religion may not be numerically strong, but it has exerted an immense influence on Christianity and Islam, as well as on Western culture as a whole. Israel is the only nation in which Judaism has a direct political authority. However, the indirect social and political influence of Judaism in the United States is widely acknowledged.

Christianity

The Christian religion began with Jesus, a first-century Palestinian Jew (4 B.C.E.– 29 C.E.). Jesus felt called and anointed by God to give himself to a ministry of teaching, preaching, and healing. His ministry led to opposition and his consequent crucifixion by the Romans. His followers/disciples took up his cause, and, along with Paul, successfully introduced a faith that was at first considered a Jewish sect into the Greco-Roman world of the first century.

Christianity encouraged people to repent (be sorry for) their sin and trust in God's love (often called "justification by faith"). The primary story of Christianity is that of Jesus, in whom God came into the world. This story gave rise to the central doctrine of Christianity, the incarnation, which affirms that God is revealed in Jesus in a unique way. The ethics of Christianity largely stem from Jesus' emphasis on love for others, in which self-giving love (*agape* in Greek) is the norm. Jesus embraced the Ten Commandments, and expanded them by calling for love of enemies and persecutors. The most important rituals of Christianity are the Lord's Supper (Communion/the Mass) and Baptism. Because of its numerical strength, Christianity has maintained a strong social dimension; in some Western nations it has exerted a powerful influence on the state.

Islam

The Islamic religion began with Muhammad, a native of what is today Saudi Arabia. He lived from 570 to 632 C.E. As a young man he received a series of revelations from God (Allah in Arabic) through the angel Gabriel, which were subsequently recorded in the *Qur'an* (Koran in English), the scriptures of Islam. Muhammad called on people to submit to God—a Muslim by definition is one who submits to God. After Muhammad's death, the Arabs who embraced his message took it to other areas of the Middle East, Africa, Europe, and Asia. Islam believes that through prayer it is possible to establish a close relationship with God. The basic story of Islam is that of Muhammad, who became the messenger of God and the seal of the prophets, who include Jewish prophets as well as Jesus. Doctrinally, Muslims believe that there is only one God, that angels are messengers of God, that God speaks through prophets, that the Koran is the word of God, and that there is life after death in either paradise or hell. The ethics of Islam are largely based on the Koran. There are five central rituals in Islam, called the Five Pillars: prayer five times a day, fasting during the month of Ramadan, almsgiving, pilgrimage to Mecca, and reciting the creed, which declares that there is only one God and Muhammad is his prophet. The Islamic religion has also had a powerful social influence, and like Christianity has attempted to control the state in countries where it is dominant (e.g., Iran, Arab countries, Egypt, and Pakistan).

Hinduism

The Hindu religion has no definite founder, but is traceable to a pre-Aryan civilization in India going back to 2500 B.C.E. The Aryans, who came to India via Persia (Iran) in the second millennium B.C.E., brought with them sacred writings called the Vedas. Later, the epic poems *Bhagavad Gita* and the *Ramayana* became very popular.

Hinduism stresses the necessity of liberation, which occurs when the atman (self or soul) is united with Brahman (ultimate reality/God). Liberation frees one from continuing incarnations. Three main yogas, or paths, help one attain liberation: jnana, karma, and bhakti. The Hindu religion contains numerous stories of gods and goddesses, who are seen as different manifestations of Brahman, the supreme god. The strongest doctrines of Hinduism have to do with liberation, reincarnation, the unreality (maya) of what is considered real (e.g., the world of space and time), and the law of karma. The idea behind this law is that people reap what they sow; they build up good karma by good actions, become good by doing good. The ethical views of Hinduism are rooted in these doctrines. Gandhi, for example, as a faithful Hindu, preached and practiced a good works (karma) yoga. The rituals of Hinduism include sacrifices to various gods, meditation, and an intense devotion to a chosen manifestation of Brahman. At times, Hindus have been content to be one among many religions existing in India, but at other times Hinduism has presented itself as *the* religion of India.

Buddhism

The religion of Buddhism was founded by a young man from India named Siddhārtha Gautama (ca. 563–ca. 483 B.C.E.), who subsequently was known as Buddha—the enlightened one. Buddha spent almost fifty years telling the people of India about his enlightenment experience and how they could have a similar experience. The story of Buddha is the primary story of this religion, but there are stories of other Buddhas and bodhisattvas (persons of compassion). Among the important doctrines of Buddhism are:

1. The Middle Path, which promotes a way between self-indulgence and self-denial.
2. The Four Noble Truths: Life is full of suffering; suffering is due to desire or craving; desire can be overcome; and practice of the eightfold path helps one overcome desire and craving.
3. The Eightfold Path consists of a series of right acts: right belief, aspiration, speech, behavior, livelihood, effort, mindfulness, and concentration. These acts can lead to nirvana, the state in which one gets rid of the false self and becomes one with what is ultimately and truly real.

The ethical dimension of Buddhism sees morality as a way of conquering desire and gaining enlightenment (steps three through five of the Eightfold Path). Because of high moral values, Buddhists denounce consumerism, murder, war, and hate. The virtue of compassion is paramount. The ritualist dimension is less elaborate than that of Hinduism, for there are no gods. The primary ritual consists of meditation. Also, even though Buddhism is a missionary religion, in that in seeks to make converts, it has refrained from imposing itself on the countries to which it has spread in both Asia and the West.

Confucianism

This religion begins with Confucius, or K'ung Fu-tzu, who lived in China between 551 and 479 B.C.E. Confucius studied the ancient Chinese classics and later gained fame as a traveling teacher. His followers took up his teachings and portrayed Confucius as an extraordinary human being. In his writings, Confucius does not come through as a religious leader, even though he apparently believed in a spiritual power behind everything, a cosmic order to which earthly order should conform. He also believed that his vocation came from this heavenly or spiritual power. This religion has many stories about Confucius and his followers. Among the important doctrines and teachings are those which have to do with not harming anyone, being benevolent to others, observing family relationships (e.g., deference of wife to husband, younger sister to older sister or brother, subject to ruler, and so forth), rulers exercising their power wisely (if they are oppressive they will lose the "mandate of heaven" which allows them to rule), and cultivating the arts that promote peace. Since many of these teachings have clear ethical connotations, it is understandable that some historians have labeled Confucianism an ethical system rather than a religion. However, there are numerous rituals in Confucianism connected to the honoring and veneration of ancestors as well as those tied to family relationships. Until recently, Confucians were very much a part of the Chinese establishment that had significant social influence. Although their power has diminished, a Confucian element is deeply embedded in Chinese culture.

Taoism

Taoism traces its origin to a semilegendary figure named Lao-tzu, who apparently lived during the time of Confucius. Since he did not teach or organize his followers, some are reluctant to accept him as the founder of a religion. Nevertheless, many Chinese have been attracted to Lao-tzu's ideas contained in the classic work entitled the *Tao-te Ching* ("Classic of the Way of Power"). Taoism stresses the need of people to align themselves with the Tao (the way), which is thought of variously as the way of ultimate reality, the way of the universe, and the way persons should order their lives so as to be in harmony with the way of the universe. The major story of Taoism is about Lao-tzu and how he wrote the *Tao-te Ching* before he left China, never to return. The major doctrines of this religion are:

1. *Wu-wei*, which roughly means actionless action, or letting things be rather than forcing them;
2. Living simply, naturally, and nonviolently;
3. *Yin-yang*, which is the practice of recognizing the complementarity of opposites and looking for the unity of opposites in a balance. Balance may be the dominant virtue of this religion.

These doctrines, as those of Confucianism, illustrate a forceful ethical dimension. A person who embodies these doctrines will be easy to get along with. Taoism does not seem to have many rituals, yet one form of Taoism has funerals that are very elaborate and very long. Taoism as a Chinese religion has not sought to have power over the state. Despite this, its influence on the Chinese people (and Westerners) continues.

Ethics within World Religions

The preceding description of world religions noted the ethical dimension in each religion. The importance of this dimension is generally accepted; all religions seem to have conduct they promote and a code to live by. Each religion provides moral guidance that a particular community of faith can stand on and embody.

In their book *How to Live Well: Ethics in the World's Religions*,[4] Denise and John Carmody compared moral views of the major world religions in four important areas: family life, work, social justice, and nature. To justify the claim that all religions have an ethical dimension, I plan to compare the views of nature in the religions we have discussed, as the Carmodys describe them. Nature is chosen over the other areas, not because it is more important, but because this area corresponds with one of the major concerns of our time. Interest in ecological and environmental issues is running high, and this comparison shows that religious ethics offers us valuable resources for dealing with one of the serious problems of our day.

Judaism as a religion has always seen creation as good, because it represents God's work. Nature is to be appreciated and enjoyed, not divinized or worshiped. Human beings were given authority over nature by God (Gen. 1:28), but were also informed that they are accountable to God for their actions. The second and older creation story (Genesis 2) has the first human beings instructed to till the garden and care for the earth. Judaism acknowledges human kinship with animals and nature. Noah took animals into the ark, supposedly to preserve all the species. Kosher laws about what animals can and cannot be eaten, and about how food is to be prepared, minimize the suffering of animals. Also, many Israeli Jews living on kibbutzim obviously live close to the land and treat it well. For the Jewish people the promised land given by God has always been a good land, "flowing with milk and honey"—a symbol of God's blessing.

The Christian religion, a child of Judaism, also appreciates creation as God's work and sees human dominion over the earth as a matter of loving stewardship, a responsibility that calls for accountability to God and careful management and caring for creation. Jesus spoke knowingly and fondly of the natural world—of flowers and trees, animals and birds. There have been Christian leaders like St. Francis of Assisi and Eastern Orthodox *starsy* (monks), who considered nature a second revelation of God. The ability to see God in all things has often been highlighted in Christian faith. Recently, a "creation-centered spirituality" has emerged within Christianity through the writings of a former Dominican priest, Matthew Fox.

The Islamic religion also speaks of creation, affirming that the world need not exist, but does so by the mercy and deliberate creation of God. Humans should cooperate with nature, so as to enable it to achieve the beauty and bounty God intended. A tenderness toward animals among Muslims has been observed. The followers of this religion also believe that God can be discerned in the natural world which God has fashioned. Concern about pollution is developing within some adherents of this religion.

In Hinduism, because all creatures are related to Brahman, all creatures are related to one another. A reverence for creation can be found in Hinduism. Hindu rituals are sacramental; they make use of such natural elements as flowers and water. The water of the Ganges River is regarded as especially sacred. A recent movement led by Hindu women in India to protect trees by hugging them provides an additional illustration of the serious concern for nature that Hinduism supports.

The Buddhist religion speaks of "the seamless connectedness" of all things. The *bodhisattva* is an ideal Buddhist, so full of compassion that he is willing to delay his own entrance into nirvana in order to assist the enlightenment of all living creatures. Buddhist rituals, especially those connected with Zen Buddhism, highlight the beauty of nature and blend the religious and the aesthetic in such things as rock gardens and flower arrangements. This religion also accepts the simple "suchness" of things, manifested in this haiku: "Evening rain,/ the banana leaf,/ speaks of it first."

Confucianism and Taoism both call for the celebration of seasons and the beauty of nature. Their cosmology sees everything as related, parts of a single organism (suggestive of the current Gaia hypothesis, which regards the universe as one large organism). The significance of the forces of nature as important actors in the human drama is acknowledged and respected by Taoists and Confucians. Taoism particularly, with its emphases on living naturally, simply, and in harmony with nature, has been lifted up by some observers as the model for an ecological religion.

The preceding paragraphs represent ideals; they do not claim that the world's living religions have an excellent record in the ways they treat nature. Members of these religions have mistreated the natural world. However, the moral ideals for a kinder, gentler approach to nature are present within these traditions, waiting to be discovered and practiced.

The above comparison of one facet of ethics within world religions need not imply that there are no differences or disagreements between religions over such moral issues as the treatment of nature, the distribution of the earth's resources, or whether war is morally permissible. The differences and conflicts between religions are real. Some of these differences are major, many are quite minor. Many of the conflicts are not about ideals, but about practices. Hindus and Christians both affirm that life is sacred and valuable. But Christians criticize Hindus about the caste system, and Hindus criticize Christians about the practice of slavery. Differences do exist, but when we compare ideals rather than practices they are not great.

Moreover, the differences between religions over morality are probably not any greater than the differences within religions themselves. Some Christians, for example, are zealously pro-life and antiabortion, others are vehemently pro-choice and accepting of abortion, to one degree or another. And the possibility of being pro-choice, yet not totally accepting of abortion except as sometimes a tragic necessity, strikes some Christians as an acceptable alternative. The same situation occurs when other moral issues arise. Sometimes I think that if Christians keep talking with one another, with greater civility and willingness to listen, they will reach agreement on weighty ethical issues. At other times I am fairly sure that disagreement and conflict is a permanent state of affairs between various Christian groups, even within the same denomination.

Another disagreement within one religion relates to a conflict over how Christian ethics should be taught. Philip Wogaman advocates the teaching of principles and guidelines for action, but Stanley Hauerwas argues that the best way to teach Christian ethics is through narratives and stories.[5] Both of these ethicists happen to be Protestant! It offers little comfort to the despairing, but let me hasten to mention that differences and disagreements among those who engage in philosophical/secular ethics are just as real. The next chapter deals with this matter.

As usual, there is another side, for despite the disagreements between and within religions over moral issues, there is larger measure of agreement than commonly recognized. There are common moral beliefs and values within living world religions. Their views on nature, family life, work, and social justice, as developed in the Carmodys' book, bear this out. There are commonalities within the ethics of world religions that call for exploration. Certainly Sissela Bok is correct when she says we need to concentrate on moral principles we find in common with people of other religions and cultures.[6] The moral crises of our time demand an emphasis on similarities rather than on differences.

The respected Catholic theologian Hans Küng, in *Global Responsibility: In Search of a New World Ethic*, investigates the common beliefs of world religions. Küng believes that a global ethic is emerging within the religious traditions of humanity. Because of these convictions he played a central role in the Parliament of the World's Religions, which met in Chicago in 1993. In this parliament, 250 global religious leaders, representing numerous religions, produced a document entitled *Declaration of a Global Ethic*. This document denounces war, poverty, sexism, unbridled capitalism, totalitarian socialism, and environmental destruction. The signers declare they have not intended to fashion a global ideology or a single unified religion, but have sought a "fundamental consensus on binding values, irrevocable standards and personal attitudes." Central to most of the world's religions, the *Declaration* observes, is some version of the Golden Rule: Do unto others as you would have them do unto you. From this general precept, they discovered "four broad ancient guidelines for moral behavior" in world religions:

1. You shall not kill (in positive terms, have respect for life).
2. You shall not steal (deal honestly and fairly).
3. You shall not lie (speak and act truthfully).

4. You shall not engage in sexual immorality (respect and love one another).[7]

A document of this nature will not readily eliminate conflicts between religious groups over ethics. It does demonstrate, however, that common ground is now being found and that the process can expand.

Having considered the matter of religious ethics, we now turn to philosophical or secular ethics, in order to understand the essential ideas and contributions of this activity.

Chapter 3

What Is Morality
(from a Philosophical Perspective)?

Religious ethics as a study began with the various religions. Philosophical ethics, or Western moral philosophy, began with the Greeks. More specifically, it began with Socrates (ca. 470–399 B.C.E.) and was further advanced by two famous successors, Plato (ca. 428–348 B.C.E.) and Aristotle (384–322 B.C.E.). Although Western moral philosophy usually makes Aristotle the dominant member of this trio, it is fair to say, as Michael Landmann does, that Socrates was the first to discuss human needs from the perspective of ethics, and by so doing paved the way for rational investigations of succeeding Greek and European philosophers.[1] Socrates was also the first to show that when we think seriously about morality, we realize that morality matters in a way that most things do not. Socrates's question as to "How should I live?" is the starting place of moral philosophy. Moreover, the question posed by Socrates in Plato's dialogue *Euthyphro* is a key question for both religious and philosophical ethics: "Do the gods command something because it is right and good, or is something right and good because the gods command it?" Socrates's question is relevant for probing the relationship between religion and morality, so we will return to it.

Philosophical ethics is an established and reputable academic discipline. As an academic field, it includes two main areas: normative ethics and metaethics. Normative ethics itself includes two branches: theoretical ethics (ethical theories) and applied ethics (an enterprise that applies normative ethics to specific moral issues, such as abortion, euthanasia, war, and so forth).

The above terms require further description. Normative ethics is the area of philosophical ethics that advances criteria, norms, and standards for making ethical judgments and decisions. It is founded on the conviction that human beings need strong beliefs about what is right and wrong, good and evil—often called values. Normative ethics also implies that people need rules, principles, and guidelines by which to live.

20

Numerous theories about the best way for making moral judgments and decisions exist. I will describe these theories by highlighting three major theories: the virtue theory, duty/obligation theory (deontological and nonconsequentialist), and good-ends theory (teleological and consequentialist). The major philosophers associated with these theories are Aristotle (virtue), Kant (duty/obligation), and Mill (good-ends). Several minor theories will be briefly treated as well.

The second area of ethics, metaethics, is quite different. The prefix *meta* means in Greek "to go beyond." Metaethics is primarily an activity in which philosophers reflect on normative ethical theories and seek to analyze moral/ethical language. What do the primary moral words—right, wrong, good, evil—really mean? This area of ethics appeals to analytic philosophers, who regard ethics as the logical study of the language of morality. The clarifications of moral language that these philosophers have achieved is appreciated, but this approach has also been criticized for failing to take into account how moral languages and communities evolve. Nevertheless, metaethics is necessary because the issue of how moral statements and assertions are justified is very important. Since this issue directly relates to the central thrust of this effort, it will be discussed later.

Most moral philosophers also consider it fruitful to distinguish between two types of ethical theories: the teleological (from the Greek *telos*, which means ends or goal) and the deontological (from the Greek *deontos*, which means duty or obligation). Teleological theories emphasize ends and consequences; deontological theories focus on doing one's duty. The primary teleological theories are egoism, utilitarianism, and possibly situationism. The primary deontological theories usually include divine command, categorical imperative, and prima facie duties. The division of ethical theories into these two types has merit, but since it neglects virtue theory, it seems to me that dealing with virtue, duty, and good-ends is appropriate.

Major Moral Theories

Virtue Theory

Virtue is often described as an inner disposition to act in morally commendable ways. The originator of this theory, Aristotle, spoke of two kinds of virtue: intellectual and moral. According to Aristotle, "moral virtue comes about as a result of habit, whence also its name (*ethike*), is one that is formed by a slight variation from the word *ethos* (habit). Moral virtues do not arise by nature, for things of nature such as stones cannot form habits contrary to their nature. Thus, neither by nature, then, nor contrary to nature do the virtues arise in us; rather we are adapted to nature to receive them, and are made perfect by habit." Aristotle further described moral virtue as the mean between excess and deficiency; as he puts it, "Virtue is a kind of mean, since, as we have seen, it aims at what is intermediate." For example, in facing danger, courage is the mean between cowardice and foolishness, and when considering giving, liberality is the mean between illiberality and prodigality.[2] Aristotle's ideas about ethics have influenced many moral philosophers.

The fact that contemporary ethicists support the spirit, if not the letter, of Aristotle's ethics, is apparent. One enthusiastic supporter of Aristotle's philosophy and ethics is Mortimer J. Adler, known for his work on *The Encyclopaedia Britannica* and the Great Books, as well as forty-plus books on diverse philosophical subjects. Adler contends for the possibility of moral knowledge, but also realizes that knowledge of moral philosophy does not make one a moral person. Echoing Aristotle, he affirms that a moral person is one who has right desires and seeks continually only that which is truly good for himself or herself.[3]

Alasdair MacIntyre, professor at the University of Notre Dame, eloquently defends Aristotle. His book *After Virtue* provoked much discussion by arguing that although Western moral philosophy has tried to go beyond virtue and Aristotle, the attempt has not been helpful. MacIntyre prefers to stay with Aristotle and Thomas Aquinas (1225–1274), a medieval philosopher/theologian who constructed a weighty theological system based on Aristotle's philosophy.

Philosophers have defended virtue ethics in various ways. Many argue that an ethics related to inner desires is better than a series of abstract principles. Richard Taylor pleads for an ethics of aspiration, as opposed to an ethics of duty. Lewis Smedes contends that considering the kind of persons we should be is more important than focusing on the right thing to do. Smedes supports an existentialist ethics of character, saying that being good, rather than simply thinking about doing good, is more appropriate. The centrality of the moral agent is crucial in virtue ethics. Individual dispositions matter a lot. Highlighting the concept of responsibility, as Peter French does, is another variation of virtue ethics. David Little refers to responsibility as the most fitting thing to undertake—it includes discernment and proper response, along with the exercising of character and virtue.[4] Interestingly, prominent Christian ethicists of recent times have also gravitated toward virtue ethics; for example, H. Richard Niebuhr, James M. Gustafson, and Stanley Hauerwas.

Aristotle also has his critics. A common criticism is that his moral philosophy is elitist, developed with the leisure class in mind. Slaves, who were abundant in ancient Greece, were regarded by Aristotle as incapable of achieving moral and intellectual virtues. Egalitarian moral philosophers find Aristotle's snobbishness unacceptable. Furthermore, the general lack of recognition of principles and duty in Aristotle's ethics makes many ethicists reluctant to embrace Aristotelian ethics without serious reservations.

Duty/Obligation Theory

Duty/obligation ethics places the emphasis on those things which humans should or ought to do ("doing the right thing") and following universal moral rules. The founder of duty ethics is the German philosopher Immanuel Kant (1724–1804). Kant wrote voluminously about different areas of philosophy, dealing cogently with metaphysics and epistemology, as well as devoting serious attention to ethics and aesthetics.

What Kant said about ethics has given rise to various interpretations, and Kantian scholars frequently argue about what Kant really meant. Nevertheless, general agreement on three main ideas of Kantian ethics prevails: The first deals with the importance of motivation, or as Kant states it, "Nothing can possibly be conceived in the world, or even out of it, which can be called good without qualification, except a good will." For Kant, this means we must act out of a sense of duty; actions done merely by inclination or self-interest are not morally good. Second, one should "act only on that maxim whereby you can at the same time will that it should become a universal moral law." This aspect of Kantian ethics, usually called the categorical imperative, implies that every human being is a rational being, capable of rationally determining which moral laws should be followed. In this context, Kant also wrote about the autonomy of the will, as opposed to heteronomy—a rule or law imposed from without. The third part of Kant's ethics is his principle on how humans should treat others: "So act as to treat humanity, whether in your own person, or that of any other, every case as end with all, never as means only."[5] Kant envisioned what he called a "kingdom of ends," a society in which all rational beings belong as ends in themselves, ruled by universal laws and moral rules. The similarity of Kant's principle on treating others as ends, not means, has often been compared by moral philosophers to the Golden Rule of Jesus.

Another salient aspect of Kant's ethics is found in his *Critique of Practical Reason,* in which he argued that human freedom, immortality of the soul, and the existence of God are three necessary postulates (reasonable although unprovable beliefs) of practical reason and the achievement of virtue and happiness. In Kant's words: "It is morally necessary to assume the existence of God."[6] Kant's insistence on absolute autonomy of the will on one hand, and the existence of a God who undergirds morality on the other, makes profoundly different interpretations of his moral philosophy understandable.

Kantian ethics has critics and defenders. The critics allege that Kant relies on reason too much and does not pay sufficient attention to the "facts" of human nature. Reason itself does not clarify the particular end humans should seek. Others claim that Kant made humans too autonomous; humans become the measure of all things, with each individual the center of the universe. Another philosopher says that the emphasis on autonomy makes humans so central that it becomes difficult for them to value animals and nature as a whole.[7] This tendency, called anthropocentrism, is widely discussed within environmental ethics. It has also been observed that Kant made humans pure thinkers; his system is very abstract. By focusing exclusively on actions and duties, Kant overlooked being and virtue.

A weighty criticism of Kant, which is relevant to the subject of this work, is that Kant made morality so much the essence of religion that he reduced religion to a product of moral consciousness, and so ended up reducing religion to mere morality.[8] In this context, many have noted that although Kant insisted on autonomy, his moral system eventually requires God, and thus brings in the very heteronomy he wanted to avoid. Furthermore, in strongly emphasizing autonomy, Kant, along with other Enlightenment figures, may have prepared the way for Nietzsche's focus on the will—the "will to power."

Kantian ethics has its zealous defenders. Kant's reliance on reason has been supported by many moral philosophers who like to think of ethics as a rational, not irrational, pursuit. Preference for autonomy abounds among secular and religious ethicists. Kant's moral philosophy also makes possible a public morality, a system of universal moral rules that all rational persons can embrace. This project was dear to the heart of Enlightenment thinkers and has not entirely lost its appeal. Furthermore, many agree that obtaining good consequences is not enough; humans have obligations even when doing them does not lead to beneficial consequences. Kant's focus on treating others as ends rather than as means also corresponds nicely with modern emphases on human dignity and freedom. And it has been noted that Kant offered a viable humanistic counterpart to Christian teaching for those no longer attracted to Christianity. In this way, Kant made room for a kind of secular faith and the modified theism that came to be called deism.[9]

Whether one agrees or disagrees with Kant, diligent students of philosophical ethics must seriously reckon with his moral philosophy. A course in philosophical ethics omitting Kant's ethical theories is hard to imagine!

Good-Ends Theory

The key figure in good-ends theories is John Stuart Mill (1806–1873), who, although much influenced by David Hume (1711–1776) and Jeremy Bentham (1748–1832), contributed most toward establishing good-ends as the basic criterion for judging moral acts. Mill himself thought his theory echoed back to Socrates. Mill's good-ends theory came to be called utilitarianism, from the principle of utility, or usefulness. The useful, in Mill's view, is that which brings pleasure and avoids pain. Happiness is identified with pleasure. In Mill's words, "The creed which accepts as the foundation of morality, Utility, or the Greatest Happiness Principle, holds that actions are right in proportion as they tend to promote happiness, wrong as they tend to produce the reverse of happiness. By happiness is intended pleasure, and the absence of pain; by unhappiness, pain and the privation of pleasure." The ultimate determiner of the rightness or wrongness of an action is its effect on happiness or pleasure. Mill did recognize, however, in contrast to Bentham, who took a quantitative approach, that "some kinds of pleasure are more desirable and valuable than others." In this context, one of Mill's most memorable statements occurs: "It is better to be a human dissatisfied than a fool satisfied; better to be a Socrates dissatisfied than a fool satisfied." Mill also argued that utilitarianism is not egoistic, for the utilitarian stand "is not the agent's own greatest happiness, but the greatest amount of happiness altogether." Further, according to Mill, one may commit harmful acts (e.g., tell a lie) to prevent greater harm. The end—happiness and pleasure—will justify the means. Lastly, Mill's view of good is that "nothing is good to human beings in so far as it is either itself pleasurable, or a means of attaining pleasure or avoiding pain."[10]

Mill also has both critics and defenders. Among the criticisms is that Mill's reasoning seems to be circular. He apparently assumes that pleasure/happiness is the desirable end because it is obviously what people desire. Mill is further criticized for equating pleasure and happiness, an equation many people dispute. Moreover, arguing that good consequences are the most important criterion for moral judgments, and that motives for acting are not all that important, opens Mill to the criticism that it is virtually impossible to be certain about the consequences of many human acts. Deontologists affirm that there are times when results are not crucial; one should do one's duty whatever the consequences.

Mill's moral theory has enthusiastic supporters. To begin with, it appeals to common sense. Achieving happiness remains an attractive goal for most people. Since most human activity is goal-oriented, emphasizing ends seems sensible. Utilitarianism also allows for human autonomy; it encourages self-reflection about what will lead to happiness for most people. Mill actually spoke of the importance of conscience. Utilitarianism deserves credit for going beyond egoism (what is good for me) by calling for altruism (what is good for as many people as possible). Utilitarianism seeks what is socially beneficial, and thus tries to remove those things which harm people and prevent them from flourishing. Utilitarianism also encourages the pursuit of equality and justice. Mill talked about each person counting as one, and no one counting as more than one. He clearly saw his theory as helpful for achieving justice, having all persons attain the happiness to which as humans they are entitled. For these reasons, utilitarianism continues as one of the dominant moral theories of our day.[11]

Moral philosophers have raised a deeper question: Should the central question of philosophical ethics be "What should I do?" or "What should I be?" Virtue theory will contend for the latter, duty and good-ends theories will argue for the former. The best answer is not easily determined. All three theories have a measure of reasonableness, offer guidance for making moral judgments and decisions, and have articulate proponents and serious followers. The temptation to say that being and doing are equally important is very human.

Additional Moral Theories

The three theories just discussed are not the whole story. Despite their general persuasiveness, one encounters further theories when investigating normative philosophical ethics. As in religious ethics, pluralism thrives. In order to do justice to the field of moral philosophy, we will look at additional theories that sometimes conflict with the three theories already discussed.

Feminist Theories

Philosophical ethics has been shaken in recent years by feminine philosophers who have shown that because Western philosophy is male-dominated, it has contributed to the oppression of women. Because of this, feminine philosophers have called for a feminist ethics.

Carol Gilligan, a Harvard University professor, is regarded as one of the founders of feminist ethics. In a writing entitled "In a Different Voice," originally appearing in 1977, she argued that for women the primary moral imperatives are caring and alleviating human suffering. In this respect women are different from the persons depicted in Lawrence Kohlberg's famous study of moral development. Kohlberg claimed that humans move from an egocentric to a societal view of what is good, and finally to universal moral rules. Women do not develop this way; they operate not in terms of principles, but by relationships, caring, and compassion.[12]

Annette Baier, of the University of Pittsburgh, in an article "What Do We Want in a Moral Theory?" says that women want what feminist philosophers provide. Feminist philosophers have concerns appreciably different from male philosophers. Baier suggests that if reflective women produce a moral theory, the guiding motif might well be one of trust, including love and loyalty, as opposed to the duty/obligation concept of typical Western moral philosophy.[13]

Another example of feminist moral philosophy comes from Sidney

Callahan, who asserts that good moral decision making engages reason and emotion in a balanced blend. Both heart and mind are essential to human wholeness, and "the most adequate moral decision-making of conscience must achieve congruence or a fusion of thinking, feeling and willing into a unified whole."[14] Callahan believes that, in ethics, philosophy and psychology ought to complement each other.

Marxist Moral Theory

Karl Marx (1818–1883) is known for his condemnation of capitalism's exploitation of the working class. If denunciation has moral implications, Marx embraced moral theory. Marx claimed, however, that his materialist philosophy of history broke "the staff of all morality." For Marx, morality and religion were forms of ideology—systems of ideas that influence human conduct. Ideologies are products of class consciousness. Morality and religion are systems of ideas that keep working people in chains. He believed that when a classless society is achieved, the new society will include what morality promised to bring about.

It can be argued that Marx did not really oppose all morality, but rather the false morality or ideology that allows human oppression. He therefore deserves credit for showing how class thinking affects moral thinking, or what MacIntyre calls moral traditions, and for pointing out that the powers of reason may deceive people, including those who argue that rationality alone can establish universal moral rules. The Marxist theory of social justice, which contends that goods should be distributed according to need, comes very close to a moral theory.

Existentialist Moral Theory

A developed existentialist moral theory is hard to find, but there are traces of existentialism within moral philosophers. The movement called existentialism began with Søren Kierkegaard (1813–1855), who strongly affirmed that being human means choosing and deciding. Kierkegaard said that humans are subjects, not the objects that science tends to make of them. There is no fixed human nature, for humans make themselves by their choices. Sartre said it thus: "What is not possible is not to choose. I can always choose, but ought to know that if I do not choose, I am still choosing."[15] Iris Murdoch pursues a similar course when noting that ethical living takes place continuously in the small moments and habits of life, for "at crucial moments of choice most of the business of choosing is already over."[16]

In philosophers dealing with ethics from an existentialist perspective, an element of antitheory is detectable. Jeffrey Blustein, for example, in *Care and Commitment*, maintains that an ethics of care is antitheory; it opposes the deductive, calculative approach to morality. Persons have values for the particular persons they are.[17]

Closely related to existentialism is the phenomenological approach. In *Toward a Phenomenological Ethics,* Werner Marx claims that he has developed a nonmetaphysical ethical theory based on awareness of mortality. This awareness makes persons realize the social nature of human existence; recognizing others as fellow mortals makes an ethics of compassion possible.[18]

Social Contract Theory

Some philosophical ethicists see social contract theory as a form of Kantian theory, but others view it as a separate theory traceable to the philosophy of Thomas Hobbes (1588–1679). Hobbes contended that governments arose in human history when humans tacitly agreed—a social contract—that strong government was necessary for stability. Humans willingly limited their individual powers to attain social order. For similar reasons, people also agreed to follow laws and moral rules, achieving a kind of "morality by agreement."

John Rawls's book *A Theory of Justice* provoked controversy. Rawls is considered a proponent of social contract, for he said that in justice as fairness "the original position of equality corresponds to the state of nature in the traditional theory of the social contract," and that "the principles of justice are chosen behind a veil of ignorance."[19]

Prima Facie Theory

The Latin phrase *prima facie* means "at first appearance" and is often used in law to refer to evidence that can be taken as fact unless it is refuted. A Scottish philosopher, W. D. Ross (1877–1971), used this term to apply to the duties and obligations persons easily recognize. For example, persons readily sense a duty to preserve life and tell the truth. When these two prima facie duties conflict, one intuitively realizes, according to Ross, that the duty to preserve life is the higher duty. Ross did not consider prima facie duties to be absolute, for they can be overridden by higher duties. Nevertheless, these duties are much more important than rules of thumb. Ross highlights six significant prima facie duties: fidelity, reparation, gratitude, justice, beneficence, and self-improvement.[20]

Egoism Theories

Two egoism theories are available, but only one is an ethical theory. Psychological egoism is a theory of human behavior that contends that humans always act out of self-interest. Ethical egoism, on the other hand, alleges that humans should promote their own well-being above everyone else's. The theory was popularized by Ayn Rand (1905–1982), a Russian-born novelist and philosopher. The work that best delineates her ideas on this matter is aptly called *The Virtue of Selfishness*. Rand believes that "man has to hold his life as a value—by choice; he has to learn to sustain it—by choice; he has to discover the values it requires and practice his virtues—by choice." And all this is accomplished by morality, which Rand defines as "a code of values accepted by choice."[21]

Natural Law Theory

This term is subject to much misunderstanding, for it suggests the laws of nature and physics by which the universe operates. In reality, the theory predates the age of science, for it goes back to Greek and Stoic philosophers who believed that there are higher laws by which people should live than the codified laws of a given society or nation. Natural law has two essential parts: The first is that by reason alone—revelation is not necessary—humans can discover and understand higher moral laws. The second is that moral duties can be derived from serious reflection on human nature and the entire natural scheme of things in which humans are placed. Human nature should be studied carefully, even scientifically. The medieval philosopher/theologian Thomas Aquinas developed a system of natural law based on Aristotle's natural teleology, in which the natural ends of human nature were emphasized. Aquinas argued that observation shows us that all humans want to live, reproduce, gain knowledge, function in society, worship God, and attain immortality. What helps humans flourish and achieve these ends is moral; what hinders these achievements is immoral. Natural law has played a significant role in Western and Roman Catholic moral philosophy. Through its emphasis on obtaining "facts" about human nature, it continues to appeal to some philosophers. Just what the "facts" of human nature are, precisely, is difficult to judge, to say nothing of the matter of going from facts to values (an issue to be considered in the next section). In anticipation of chapter 6, let me mention the possibility of natural law theory serving as a bridge between religious and philosophical ethics.

Rights Theories

An increasing human insistence on "rights" has evolved within American society. Every day we hear people talking about their rights. In *Matters of Life and Death*, John Cobb deals with the right to kill, the right to die, the right to live, and the right to love. He defends this approach by calling rights "the language in which most of the current discussion in our society occurs."[22] A right is really a claim against another; for example, a right to free speech is a claim that one should be allowed to say, or at least not prevented from saying, what one wishes. A right to education is a claim that educational opportunities should be provided. The first example is a negative right, a freedom from; the second is a positive right, a freedom to. Further, there are legal as well as moral rights; the right to vote is a legal right in most societies; the right to an education is a moral right, not always guaranteed by law.

Brenda Almond, a philosopher at the University of Hull, argues that the concept of universal human rights has roots in the natural law theory, and that an emphasis on rights has been central in the Western liberal tradition. Some conservatives object to political rights (e.g., the right to welfare), but are sympathetic to economic rights (the right to keep what one has fairly earned).

Claiming rights is not necessarily selfish, for those who assert their rights often agree that others have rights too. Rights are not incompatible with social responsibility, even if the connection is sometimes slighted. The Libertarian political party sees rights as a way of limiting governmental power. The Harvard philosopher Robert Nozick has been a strong supporter of human rights, including the right to keep what one has earned.[23]

Some moral philosophers object to the emphasis on rights. Daniel Callahan maintains that in the United States rights thinking has led to a "minimalist morality," in which the only recognized duty is that of not harming another person. No duty to help another is positively felt.[24] The Communitarian movement says that when people focus on rights they tend toward individualism and evade responsibilities to their communities. However, moral philosophers who emphasize rights generally agree that moral life cannot be described exclusively in rights language. The fact that we seem to be reaching a high level of agreement or consensus on universal human rights, demonstrated in the Universal Declaration of Human Rights, could facilitate that "common morality" that many members of the global community desire.

Responding to Diversity

The foregoing survey of moral theories, norms by which moral judgments and decisions can be made, raises questions: Why so many theories and norms? Can we handle such a confusing array of possibilities?

Three possible ways of responding to diverse moral theories are available: The first recognizes that a plurality of moral theories exists and declares that one must learn to live with this situation. It does not quite say "the more the merrier," but affirms that plurality looks for ways of combining the different theories. One takes a little from each and thus arrives at a desirable mix. Americans seem to be fond of such eclectic and syncretistic approaches. As far as I know, moral philosophers do not advocate such a facile combination of diverse moral theories.

The second approach, represented by Alasdair MacIntyre, maintains that the moral theories of Western philosophical ethics are incommensurate. We have no reliable way of comparing and judging these theories; no overarching criteria for measuring their adequacy are available. Many moral philosophers agree that we have no good ways for resolving the inevitable conflicts.

The third approach is taken by those not comfortable with the first two approaches, by philosophers not content with an easy eclecticism or a dogmatic declaration that no common ground can be found. The fact that consensus is not readily achieved is quickly acknowledged, but the search for agreement is truly worthwhile.

Issues in Philosophical Ethics

Pluralism in moral theories is one part of the complexity of philosophical ethics; another part relates to a series of questions moral philosophers have raised and tried to answer. Since these questions and their possible answers have a significant bearing on the underlying thesis of this work, I will deal with four that seem to be especially relevant to a relational approach to morality.

Do Moral Theories Presuppose a View of Human Nature?

Moral philosophers often ask whether humans are free or determined. Are humans free enough to be morally responsible or capable of acting unselfishly? This question shows that moral philosophy has to deal with human nature, the way we are. Is it possible to have a moral theory that does not imply a view of human nature?

The answers given by moral philosophers vary. Among the three central figures of philosophical ethics—Aristotle, Kant, and Mill—only Aristotle explicitly recognizes the importance of human nature in practicing moral philosophy. Modern philosophers working in the analytical tradition seldom consider a philosophy of human nature necessary; for them analyzing and clarifying moral language is sufficient.

Some moral philosophers acknowledge the relevance of a philosophy of human nature for their enterprise and further recognize the value of psychology for dealing with human nature. As the study of the soul/self/mind, psychology was seen by Plato and Aristotle as a part of philosophy. Sidney Callahan affirms that a full account of human activity, making use of philosophy and psychology, is helpful in moral philosophy.

Owen Flanagan further contends that there is no single type of moral personality. Only through psychology is it possible to develop an accurate theory of human nature.[25] A psychoanalyst and ethics professor at Syracuse University, Ernest Wallwuk, in a book on psychoanalysis and ethics, contends that Freud's view of human beings provides an adequate basis for moral theory.[26]

Philosophical anthropology emerged and is an area of philosophy that has taken root in the United States. It focuses on human nature as the central philosophical concern. Philosophical anthropologists have attempted to take a fresh approach to human nature; their insights are interesting and helpful. For example, Michael Landmann declares that humans create culture and are also created by culture, an observation that confirms MacIntyre's contention that all moral reasoning occurs within particular traditions.[27]

If humans create culture, then to some extent humans also create morality. I agree with James M. Gustafson, who says it is important to begin ethical reflection at the point of human existence, for people are not pure thinkers, but existing individuals. Many moral philosophers realize that moral theories presuppose a view of human nature. Behind moral theories one can often discover theories of human nature.

Do Moral Theories
Imply a View of Reality?

This question grows out of the previous one, for a view of human nature is one aspect of a person's view of reality as a whole. The question here is whether moral theory implies a metaphysical position, a worldview. Before responding, some clarifications may be helpful.

If reality is that which is real, a view of reality is that which a person truly considers real. The real can refer to that which one can handle with the five senses. The real can also apply to things not encountered by our senses—ideas, ideals, and values such as truth, beauty, and goodness, as well as things that are right and good, loving and just. A view of reality can embrace all of the above and more.

A metaphysical position refers to a view of reality—"the conceptual picture underlying one's world picture," or "a general map of how the world is and can possibly be."[28] A worldview is similar, for it is one's way of seeing and understanding the world, a vision of life as a whole. Michael Landmann says that every person has a comprehensive worldview, or *Weltanschauung* (a way of looking at the world), prior to every philosophy.[29] Worldviews are not shaped in a vacuum, in isolation from others. People develop their beliefs about the world/universe according to what they perceive are the beliefs of the groups to which they belong or want to belong. Our worldviews and underlying assumptions about the world influence us greatly.

Iris Murdoch's book *Metaphysics as a Guide to Morals* reveals an important idea: our metaphysics (views of reality or worldviews) influence and guide our moral beliefs and action. Murdoch sees human consciousness as the fundamental mode of functioning as a moral being, and maintains that "in many familiar ways values pervade and color what we take to be the reality of our world." She asks, "If we reflect about moral values can we avoid picturing the world?" for "moral energy is a function of how I understand, see the world."[30] Murdoch's ideas give a convincing affirmative response to the question posed.

In an address before an annual meeting of the Society of Christian Philosophers, Louis P. Pojman argued that the moral philosophies of Aristotle and Kant reflect views of reality, a worldview. He sees a kind of vertical metaphysics at work in their philosophies. In Aristotle, vertical metaphysics is found in three ways: a common human nature, which gives humans a definite end and purpose; the human ability to reason, which makes humans different; and the view that because humans can reason they can become like the gods, enjoying a life of contemplation.

Pojman also detects a vertical metaphysics in Kant, for he shoved God out the front door only to bring God back in by the rear door. Kant wanted ethics and humans to be autonomous. He desired an ethical system that had no need of a divine lawgiver. But as Aristotle before him, Kant had a metaphysical view of human nature; he believed that humans are the end of creation, rational selves grounded in God. Kant's view of persons as ends in themselves is rooted in the idea of a transcendent self. Kant also spoke of complete good (*bonum consummatum*) as the time when virtue is rewarded. Since this does not happen during earthly life, God and immortality are needed.

Even though Pojman does not deal with a vertical metaphysics, I believe one is present in Mill. Mill says that the transcendental ethical virtue of justice is supported by his moral philosophy. He also makes conscience the internal sanction for his moral theory. More importantly, Mill makes happiness the ultimate end, without saying why it is the ultimate end. He apparently concludes that what is desired is desirable—thus happiness is desirable because happiness is desirable! Like Kant, Mill ends with a postulate.

It seems to me that those moral philosophers are correct who argue that moral theories presuppose and incorporate views of reality, or worldviews. If human language contains "a hidden metaphysics," as Benjamin Whorf argued persuasively sometime back, moral philosophy also has a metaphysics, sometimes hidden, sometimes plainly seen. And if this is so, a relationship between religion and morality is certainly possible.

Can Moral Beliefs
Be Adequately Justified?

This question may be the most complex. How do we find adequate grounding and justification for our deepest moral beliefs? This question calls on persons who advance theories and criteria for making moral judgments to defend and justify their views and provide salient reasons why their moral theories are acceptable.

As I see it, this profound question breaks down into four related questions: (1) Is moral knowledge/truth possible and attainable? (2) Is reason an adequate justification for moral beliefs? (3) Is science an acceptable grounding for moral theories? (4) Is a noncircular answer possible to the question, Why should I be moral?

1. *Is moral knowledge/truth possible and attainable?* As expected, moral philosophers disagree on the answer. There are philosophical ethicists who refer to themselves as "cognitivists" (from the Greek *gnonai* and the Latin *cognoscere*, which both mean "to know"). Some cognitivists maintain that from a study of the natural world, and the facts learned from such a study, moral judgments can be made. It is possible, say these philosophers, to go from an *is* to an *ought* (more on this later). Philosophers who take this position are called naturalists, and include figures like Aristotle, Bentham, Ralph Barton Perry, and Mortimer J. Adler.

There are cognitivists, however, who point to intuition rather than natural facts as the source of moral knowledge. Their view is that moral knowledge is not gained through sensory investigation but through a direct awareness of self-evident moral truth. Among philosophical ethicists espousing this position are G. E. Moore, W. D. Ross, and A. C. Ewing.

At the other extreme, one finds moral philosophers who call themselves noncognitivists. Moral standards, they believe, do not express a state of affairs; they express only strong emotions and attitudes about the rightness and wrongness of certain actions. Alfred J. Ayer and Charles L. Stevenson represent the noncognitive approach. These philosophers do, however, maintain that reason plays an important role in making moral judgments.

It must also be noted that there are moral philosophers who place themselves between the cognitivists and noncognitivists. R. M. Hare, for example, says that moral statements are prescriptive action guides that one must be able to defend with good reasons, and that a person must decide on a way of life that is truly desirable. Philippa Foot, another British moral philosopher who is not a naturalist, nevertheless argues for a close relation between facts and values. A person can recognize the moral value of courage in another person, says Foot, even if the valuing person is a coward.[31]

The question of whether knowledge is possible is closely allied to the branch of philosophy called epistemology (from the Greek *episteme,* which means knowledge or understanding). Epistemology seeks to answer the questions of what and how we know. In general, philosophers have answered by saying that there are two major sources of knowledge, senses and reason, and two minor sources, intuition and authority. If Midgley is correct in noting that moral judgment of some kind is a necessary element in our thinking or knowing, and Louden is right in contending that morality is embedded in all human cognitive efforts, then all four sources should help persons gain knowledge and truth. In pursuing this claim, we will consider these four sources briefly.

Senses: We have alluded to the naturalist cognitivists, who believe that by careful study of what is, one can arrive at moral judgments. This view goes back to Aristotle and has been supported by moral philosophers over the centuries. Adler, as noted, argues that reason is not enough. Moral philosophy needs the facts of human nature. Adler further claims that whatever we truly need, such as food, clothing, and shelter, is really good for us. Humans should therefore desire what is really good for them. Adler sees the desire to seek what is really good a self-evident prescriptive judgment.

Reason: Since the next question deals with the adequacy of reason as justification for moral beliefs, my only comment here is that virtually all moral philosophers agree that reason is one of the essential sources of moral knowledge. Continuing interest in Plato's emphasis on seeking the highest idea, that of good or goodness, confirms the role of reason as a source of moral knowledge.

Intuition: A minor source of knowledge for most philosophers, some philosophical ethicists nevertheless have considered intuition, as a direct awareness of moral truth, a valuable source of moral knowledge. Murdoch refers repeatedly to the importance of consciousness and imagination in moral thinking. Other philosophers, including our third president, Thomas Jefferson (the first president of the American Philosophical Society), have spoken of an inner moral sense. In *The Moral Sense,* James Q. Wilson claims that humans indeed have a moral sense.[32] Just where this moral sense is located and whether it is related to nature or nurture are further questions.

The ancient and somewhat continuing belief in conscience as an inner sense of what is right and wrong seems fairly close to intuition. However, because social scientists have strongly argued that conscience is largely a product of social conditioning, modern moral philosophers rarely promote conscience as a path to moral knowledge.

Authority: The fourth source of knowledge is that which we learn from authorities, from those who know more than we do. This source is seldom considered favorably by philosophers, who maintain that knowledge should be firsthand, acquired through one's own senses and reason. But we can ask: Do we not frequently rely on authorities we trust to give us scientific and historical knowledge? Certainly, anyone serious about ethics can learn much from studying the writings of the great moral philosophers. If it is ridiculous to reinvent the wheel, it seems equally foolish to reinvent Aristotle, Kant, and Mill.

The question of whether moral knowledge is possible to attain remains central within philosophical ethics. If moral knowledge is impossible, it is difficult to imagine how people will make moral judgments and answer the two primary moral questions: What should I do? What should I be? If moral knowledge is totally unattainable, meaningful moral discourse cannot take place.

2. *Is reason an adequate justification for our deepest moral beliefs?* The key word in this question is adequate, for we have already noted the impossibility of attaining moral knowledge without the help of reason. The word adequate suggests sufficiency, that reason is all we need. Here again moral philosophers disagree. Most of them agree that reason is one way of justifying moral judgments; making reason the only way is debatable.

Philosophers who espouse reason as adequate and sufficient can be found. The late scientist/philosopher Isaac Asimov once said that "there is nothing else to trust than reason." Moral philosophers have often pushed reason as entirely adequate for justifying moral judgments. David Gauthier believes that moral principles are principles of "rational choice." Bernard Gert suggests that morality is a public system that all impartial rational persons will embrace in order to govern the behavior of rational beings. Ronald Green argues that moral reason presupposes freedom and autonomy; to oppose reason is to oppose freedom. David Brink highlights the role of reason by contending that moral theories can be evaluated on the basis of their coherence with our other beliefs. In doing this, morality goes beyond subjectivity and becomes objective. Aristotle, Kant, and Mill apparently saw reason as capable of understanding what is truly moral.[33]

Moral philosophers who do not believe that reason is as adequate and sufficient as the above philosophers do accept the importance of reason. Reason is regarded by most moral philosophers as the means by which it is possible to justify moral beliefs and reach understanding. A. Phillips Griffiths contends that in order to have moral discourse at least some moral principles must be accepted as rationally acceptable.[34] A rational basis for ethics makes it possible to make rational moral choices.

Some ethicists place great emphasis on reason. William Frankena, for example, says that since moral philosophers desire to achieve a rational morality, believing in moral principles is rationally justifiable. Frankena maintains that it is unnecessary to ask why one should be rational, for in requesting reasons one has already committed oneself to being rational. To ask why one should be rational implies that one is willing (or at least should be) to exercise reason.[35] Michael Perry also seems to be correct in alleging that one cannot intelligently question the use of reason unless its use is already presupposed. If we ask for reasons, we must be willing to look at reasons.[36] These ideas may also pertain when we ask, Why should I be moral?

Before considering some arguments against reason as an adequate justification for moral judgments, let us recall that religion and religious ethics are favorably disposed to the employment of reason. Theologians and philosophers are often very close in embracing reason as a crucial element of being human; both use reason in pursuing their respective purposes. On the other hand, the fact that some moral philosophers have been negative about reason as the way to justify moral beliefs cannot be ignored. Moral philosophers negative about reason make several pertinent points.

First, they point to the other ways in which moral judgments and actions are determined. Anthony Cortese claims that morality is more socially constructed than constructed by rational moral principles or the structures of human cognition.[37] Moral philosophers frequently use approaches that go beyond the usual dimensions of reason. Martha Nussbaum, for example, shows that stories contain valuable truths about human life; the emotional may be just as important as the intellectual in moral thinking.[38] Robert Coles has used novels and poetry very effectively in helping future physicians in the Harvard Medical School deal with moral questions. Edward Long suggests that the discernment process, which is both rational and affective, is important in moral reflection.[39] And John Roth actually advocates a moral language that is lyrical and poetic rather than rational and intellectual.[40] Images and imagination may be more helpful in moral thinking than concepts and reasoning. Probably only a minority make moral decisions in rational and deductive ways.

Second, moral philosophers point out that reason may have very little to do with moral motivations and action. Reason operates separately from the human motivation to do what is right and good. Practical reason—figuring out how to get what one wants—can be used to accomplish great evil as well as great good. Kant's observation about the unqualified priority of a good will is still sound. Reason alone will not indicate the end we should seek. We cannot reason ourselves into moral sentiments. James W. Fowler adds that reason is not sufficient to make us act; inner dispositions are needed before human action takes place.[41] Morality is more a matter of doing and being than of cogitation and reasoning.

Third, moral philosophers not totally enamored with reason point to the fact that reason is incapable of resolving conflicts between moral theories. MacIntyre's thesis that reason cannot bring different moral views into agreement may be right; rational principles do not resolve conflicts. Rationality does not remove partiality. Leslie Newbigin notes that we cannot rationally criticize a truth claim except on the basis of some truth claim accepted without question.[42] He cites Michael Polanyi as one of the first scientists and philosophers to call attention to the inevitable subjective element in all knowing; pure objectivity or rationality is probably nonexistent, for all human knowledge involves the commitments of fallible human beings.

Fourth, moral philosophers stressing the limits of reason also realize that reason can be misused. Rationality can lead to rationalization, reasoning ourselves into thinking and doing as we wish. Freud showed that the human capacity for self-deception is rather powerful. MacIntyre has argued that there are competing and contradictory understandings of rationality. Therefore, as Gamwell affirms, all theories of rationality should be open to question.[43] It is difficult to be fully rational in a world that contains so many competing ideologies.

Fifth, moral philosophers distrusting reason point out that reason seldom stands alone; reason depends on communities, traditions, and worldviews (metaphysics). A pure rationality without any presuppositions does not exist. As D. Z. Phillips says, "We do not have reasons for our values, our values are our reasons."[44] Ethical reasoning derives from surrounding cultures; all reasoning is in fact somewhat culturally conditioned. Feminist philosophers agree, noting that what we call logic often carries a load of values. The sociologist James Davidson Hunter observes that people live in moral communities that have an ultimacy for their members.[45] The fact that moral judgments are somewhat dependent on culture and tradition shows the correctness of what some call "cultural relativism" (not the same as moral relativism). In light of the above arguments, it seems fair to conclude that while reason is greatly needed, it is not a totally adequate and sufficient source for justifying moral judgments and decisions.

3. *Is science an adequate grounding/justification for our deepest moral theories?* This question is really two questions: Does science give us facts about humans who engage in moral activity? and, Is it possible to move from scientific facts to values, from the *is* to the *ought*, from description to prescription? Both questions are relevant to an assessment of the role of science in morality and ethics. The first question is somewhat complicated, for there are at least five ways in which it can be answered.

First, ethics has often been regarded as a science. Some of the definitions of the *Oxford English Dictionary* so indicate. An article in the *Encyclopaedia Britannica* declares that ethics is a "normative science." Frankena argues that as scientists do their thinking independent of tradition and culture (a debatable point), moral philosophers likewise see ethics as a science.[46] Viewing ethics as a science appeals to those wishing to make ethics more objective.

Second, science as an enterprise has its own values. Many scientific concepts reflect moral values. Robert Louden claims that science presupposes a commitment to basic moral values, such as honesty and truthfulness.[47]

Third, science has explanations for morality; sociobiologists maintain that altruism is genetically determined, that evolution produced beings capable of morality. A key figure in this area, E. O. Wilson, claims that a complete neural understanding is a firm basis for ethics.[48] This view places morality within the program of the brain. It should be added that there are many who will debate these views.

Fourth, science can be helpful for morality. Biology, for example, helps us to know more about humans. A prominent bioethicist acknowledges that ethics needs science, and that the bioethics that relies on biology and humanistic knowledge provides a constructive pattern for survival.[49] Science can help us understand the constraints within human behavior and thus contribute to the worldview in which our moral decisions are made. Many ethicists admit that they need empirical facts in order to make moral judgments. As noted, Gustafson is convinced that empirical science can help us describe human life in religiously neutral terms. One example of how science helps ethics relates to the environment—in making the public more aware of environmental degradation, scientists stimulated the emergence of environmental ethics.

Fifth, science itself is changing in positive ways; the "new paradigms" of science and theology have been observed. Scientists today are less mechanistic and more organic or ecological in their approach. This approach, in turn, enables us to see all forms of life, including human, as parts of an organism in which all the parts are interconnected. It also fosters a less individualistic attitude, another contribution to moral thinking.

Naturally, moral philosophers exist who do not regard science so favorably. They contend that if science wants to be value-free (and scientists do not agree on this), then scientists cannot help humans live well. They also point out that scientists frequently disagree; for example, not all biologists see genes as completely determinative. John Searle is very critical of the cognitive sciences and their claims and argues that the idea of the brain as a computer is only a metaphor. Searle does not think that science deals adequately with human consciousness.[50] A respected social scientist, Robert Wuthnow, says we must remember that science itself is a social construction and that implied beliefs and values often affect the ways scientific research is conducted.[51] Prior commitments and experience often influence a scientist's selection of relevant facts.

Strong anti–science/technology attitudes can be found. Robert Pirsig, for example, contends that because science in its value-free mode makes no provision for morality, the moral problems of our day are actually caused by science. The popularity of science and its inability to deal with values creates problems. Pirsig wants to make values, not facts and things, the center of reality.[52]

Our first question about the role of science in ethics relates to whether science gives us facts about human nature that can be used for constructing moral theories. We have noted that several moral philosophers are convinced that science provides a factual basis for moral ideas and beliefs. Aristotle's virtue ethics, along with natural law theory, regards facts about human nature as clear and definite. However, what is regarded as a fact can be influenced by the prior values and commitment of the observer. Facts are extremely susceptible to interpretation and evaluation, and are by themselves rather "empty" until interpreted. The fact that humans kill members of their own species is seen by some as evidence that violence and aggression are innate. Others argue that they cannot be innate because they are not universal. Science may indeed give us facts about human nature, but since facts have to be squared with all the elements of human experience (the coherence test), what facts really mean remains debatable.

The other question relative to the role of science in ethics is whether one can go from facts to values, from an *is* to an *ought*, from description to prescription. As it is a continuing issue in moral philosophy, protagonists for opposing viewpoints abound. The negative response has been strong. This response, credited to David Hume, has insisted that one cannot go from an *is* to an *ought*. The fact that people cheat each other does not imply they should, nor does the fact that people are kind to each other imply they ought to be kind. The jump from description to prescription is a big one. G. E. Moore named this jump the "naturalistic fallacy," and the name has stuck.

But there is another side. The above approach makes science a value-free activity. Science, however, does have its own built-in values, accepted by many scientists. Callahan and Engelhardt affirm that there is no crisp line between explanation and evaluation. They are convinced that science and values are not mutually exclusive, and wish to eliminate value-free science and science-free values.[53] Moving from facts to values, and back again, is possible. We often use factual statements to back up moral standards. Louden declares that to say we cannot derive an *ought* from an *is*, is a form of moral skepticism, denying that moral knowledge is attainable.[54] These questions are significant, for if science does not provide facts about human beings, and if facts cannot lead to values, science becomes totally incapable of proving justification for moral beliefs. If science can contribute to metaphysical and religious beliefs, it can also contribute to moral beliefs. The contribution of science to environmental ethics convinces me that science has a role in ethics.

4. *Is a noncircular answer possible to the question of why I should be moral?* Another part of the justification issue, this question is not whether morality is necessary, but why I should be moral—a personal, existentialist kind of question.

Naturally, this question can be asked with different intentions. It can be asked cynically as well as sincerely and conscientiously. It is raised here in the second sense, as a question that cuts to the very heart of justifying our basic moral convictions—just why we believe we should do what is right and good or be persons of virtue. The question has the ring of ultimacy, for it inquires into our fundamental reasons for being moral people. The foremost philosopher of moral development, Lawrence Kohlberg, said that on the highest level of moral development one asks this very question, and then realizes that it is similar to asking, Why live? or, How should I face death? Real moral maturity requires a genuine understanding of the meaning of life.[55]

Some answers to this question are definitely inadequate: To say that one should be moral because it pays will not do. One can easily show that being moral does not always pay. Moral behavior frequently goes without a reward. Or to say that one should be moral because it leads to happiness or flourishing is inadequate, for again it may not happen as expected. And to fall back on saying that I should be moral just because I should be, is circular. Is Perry right in contending that there is no noncircular way to answer this question?[56] Perhaps raising the question provides its own answer. At any rate, the question is one humans cannot forever evade.

Is a Common Morality Possible?

Because this particular issue bears a close relation to later conclusions, it is mentioned here as the last of four issues in philosophical ethics. The question is whether a moral consensus, a common moral vocabulary, a world or global ethic, is achievable. Interest in this possibility seems to be keen. And the answers of moral philosophers go from one end of the spectrum to the other.

Probably the best-known moral philosopher to advocate a common morality was Immanuel Kant. As an Enlightenment figure, Kant shared the Enlightenment ideal of humans eventually learning to live in peace by following those universal moral rules which human rationality enables them to understand. Philosophical ethicists who accept Kant's theories tend to agree. Even some philosophers not Kantian in approach believe that a common morality is possible. Mortimer J. Adler predicts that in time we will overcome the illusion of thinking that there is a Western mind and an Eastern mind, and realize that "there is only a human mind and it is one and the same for all human beings." Adler is fond of speaking about "trans-cultural truth."[57]

People in other fields think a common morality is possible. James Q. Wilson argues that empirical findings point to a core of near-universal moral beliefs, a shared moral sense.[58] Moral philosophers can and should seek common moral ground. As we have seen, the Parliament of the World's Religions produced "a global ethic."

Moral philosophers differ on this one too. A recent book by Gene Outka and John P. Reeder Jr., entitled *Prospects for a Common Morality*, begins by saying that "recent moral and political thought seems Janus-faced."[59] On one hand there is confidence that a cross-cultural consensus on moral beliefs, which will provide humanity a common morality, will emerge. A lack of confidence in such a prospect is also evident. The essayists in this book are almost equally divided between those who have and those who lack confidence in a common morality. This issue is also compounded by an apparent contemporary situation: the universal principles and values needed by a global ethic mightily conflict with the strong desire of different groups for their own ethnic and cultural identity. Despite this, the necessity and desirability of a common morality continues to be a strong concern.

Concluding Comments

This chapter on philosophical ethics has been considerably longer than the one on religious ethics. This does not imply that philosophical ethics is more important. I believe that religious and philosophical ethics are of almost equal value in helping us deal with the moral issues of our day.

Our discussion of philosophical ethics prompts two related conclusions: there is as much variety in philosophical ethics as there is in religious ethics, and there is as much conflict and disagreement in philosophical ethics as within religious ethics.

It is possible that the disagreements within philosophical ethics have been overdrawn, but I have tried to be fair. In addition to the three main theories of normative philosophical ethics—virtue, duty/obligation, and good-ends—other theories have been discussed. We also considered four pressing issues in moral philosophy and here, too, noted disagreements. I do not completely share MacIntyre's dismal conclusion about incommensurability within moral philosophy, but the presence of conflicts is obvious. Perhaps some of the disagreement is actually healthy!

To conclude our discussion on religious ethics, we pursued commonalities and agreements. Let me attempt the same for philosophical ethics by highlighting seven points of agreement among ethicists who engage in serious moral reflection from a nonreligious perspective:

1. They believe that some moral knowledge/truth is possible. In contrast to the moral skeptics, moral philosophers believe that some measure of moral wisdom is achievable. Without this belief they would not make the serious efforts they make.

2. They are concerned with both the right and the good, basic words within a moral vocabulary. No matter how difficult defining these words may be, they do have meaning for moral philosophers as well as for the lay person.

3. They recognize that the central questions, How should I live? and, What does it mean to live well? are important human questions and concerns.

4. They generally subscribe to such basic moral principles as nonmaleficence and beneficence: We should not harm other people (or animals and plants), but should do good to as many creatures as possible.

5. They agree that murder, theft, greed, dishonesty, lying, injustice, selfishness, and so on are morally reprehensible, and that their opposites are morally commendable. Specific moral practices are what the abstract thing we call morality is really all about.

6. They believe that humans should be free to choose how they will live, what kind of persons they will be, and what rules and principles they will follow. Morality/ethics should be a self-chosen way of life. Although autonomy has its limits, it is very important for moral philosophers.

7. They agree that people should be able to give some reasons for their moral beliefs, for acting as they do, and for why they are the kind of people they are. Moral philosophers differ greatly according to the faith they have in reason, but almost all of them have some faith in reason as a beneficial human capacity.

In ending this discussion of philosophical ethics, I wish to reaffirm my belief in the value of both religious and philosophical ethics. I am persuaded that these two central ways of being moral and searching for moral wisdom will continue, and I am further convinced that it would be wise for religious and philosophical ethicists to acknowledge and understand each other. Since this conviction is relevant to my general conclusion, I will not defend it here, but proceed to discuss the three major ways in which religion and morality, religious and philosophical ethics, can deal with each other.

Chapter 4

Religion and Morality Are Inseparable

The first option to consider for how religion and morality should deal with each other calls for inseparability—they should not be separated. There are variations within this view: There are those who would argue for a total inseparability, and claim that we cannot have religion without morality or morality without religion. Then there are those who would say that because religion and morality are so close in their interests they should never be completely separated.

The word dependent is frequently used by those arguing for inseparability. I refrain from using this word because it is misleading. Some maintain that morality depends on religion, others that religion depends on morality. Either dependency makes them difficult to separate. The word "inseparable" suggests more of a mutual dependence, rather than having one completely depend on the other. While many promote the dependence of morality on religion, or the dependence of religion on morality, the question of which one depends on the other seems fruitless and unhelpful.

The primary effort of this chapter is that of looking at several arguments for religion and morality's being inseparable. It concludes with a selection of notable quotations that support this option. I will not criticize this approach here, for the following chapter, which argues for the merit of completely separating religion and morality, fulfills this purpose.

The Way Faith Works

Within Western religions, a person of religious faith wishes to show gratitude and love to God, to please God and do God's will. These faith attitudes lead naturally into morality, into being good persons and doing what is considered right and good. Gratitude to God serves as the motive for being moral. A Jewish theologian, Albert Friedlander, believes that true revelatory experiences of mystery contain ethical implications.[1] The prophets of the Jewish Bible furnish dramatic examples of religious experience issuing in moral convictions. Henry David Aiken rightly observes that for people of religious faith God is good by definition, and believers are reluctant to presume for themselves the complete nature of good and evil—they want God to authorize their activities in the realm of morality.[2] Humans live their relationship with God in both religious and moral ways. Separating morality from religion seems artificial.

Indeed, for most religious people religion and morality are too close to separate. In the Islamic religion, giving alms to the poor is both religious and moral. Larry Shinn says that it is doubtful that a religious ethic can be maintained without religious experience. Many moral saints, such as Gandhi and Mother Teresa, are religious saints also. It is incorrect to say that all religious believers are morally exemplary persons, or that unbelievers have no moral qualities (a point to which we shall return), but that religious faith can lead to the practice of moral virtues seems indisputable.

Religions Have a Moral Element

Morality as one of the dimensions of world religions has been noted. Religions without moral teachings are rare, and probably nonexistent. The world religions described in chapter 2 definitely have a moral dimension. In most descriptions of religion this dimension is included, if not emphasized. Mortimer J. Adler, for example, is convinced that all religions have moral prescriptions that presuppose religious beliefs. Larry Shinn maintains that all religious traditions display an intense interest in behavioral conformity with the expressed goals of the tradition.[3] A religion that fails to embrace and embody moral values lacks credibility. We use the word hypocrite to refer to people of religious faith whose morality does not match their religious profession.

Western Religions
Emphasize Inseparability

Within the Western religions of Judaism, Christianity, and Islam, religion and morality are considered inseparable. In both Judaism and Christianity, God's commands and directions often have a strong moral ring. In Judaism the inseparability of religion and morality is illustrated in the prophetic writings of the Jewish Bible. Prophets such as Amos, Isaiah, Micah, and others taught that God is holy and just, and thus expected people covenanted with God to be just and honest in their relations with one another. The way they treated others—morality—was a way of honoring God—religion. For religious Jews, religious faith is the source of morality.

In Christianity, the inseparability of religion and morality is also evident. Many people have actually regarded the founder of Christianity as more a teacher of morality than a religious leader or Messiah. Thomas Jefferson saw Jesus as a moral teacher, not a savior. In reality, Jesus did not separate his religious and moral teachings. He taught that the two greatest commandments were to love God and to love your neighbor (Matt. 22:36–40). Jesus did not separate these commandments. And since love to God can be seen as religion, and love to neighbor can be viewed as morality, Jesus followed the Jewish prophetic tradition of uniting religion and morality. Christians have consistently emphasized the organic unity of morality and religion. Wolfhart Pannenberg declares that Christian ethics begins with accepting the reality of God and living in accordance with that reality, an acceptance that certainly embraces what Jesus said and did.[4] Moreover, some Christian theologians and ethicists, such as Dietrich Bonhoeffer, have contended that Christian ethics is entirely different from moral philosophy, thus highlighting the very close relationship of Christian faith and Christian morality. Christians regard God, not themselves, as the source of their moral values.

The Islamic religion includes many Jewish and Christian insights. Its founder Muhammad also taught that Allah, or God, expects believers to walk "a straight path." A Muslim by definition is one who submits to God and follows God's will in all of his or her activities. For Islam also, the fact of its adherents' reluctance to separate church (religion) and state further demonstrates the inseparability of religion and morality in this religion.

Eastern religions have not been mentioned here, because these religions do not focus on a personal God whose will is to be sought and followed. Instead, Eastern religions focus on ultimate reality, or the unconditional. This element of ultimacy present in Eastern religions is seen in concepts like Brahman, nirvana, and the Tao, from Hinduism, Buddhism, and Taoism, respectively. Views of ultimacy can and do influence ways of living. Eastern religions have their distinctive approach, but the possibility of a close relationship between religion and morality does exist within these religions.

Religious Beliefs Shape Behavior

Religions shape the ways people behave. A religion professor, John K. Simmons, has invented the formula B + B = B, to capture this truth: Beliefs + Believers = Behavior.[5] Many persons derive their moral values from religion. I am not claiming that religion is the only source of moral beliefs and behavior, simply that religion has been, and continues to be, a powerful influence in shaping human behavior. Religious believers practice moral teachings, and demonstrate private and public virtues, because of their loyalty to a transcendent reality. John F. Haught alleges that there is no persistent ethical enthusiasm unless one really believes.[6] William Frankena, a moral philosopher who regards religion and morality as separate, does say that though not logically entailed, it is "reasonable" to claim that if God is love, those who sincerely believe this will feel constrained to love.[7]

Human Freedom
to Seek Moral Wisdom

If humans are free and autonomous, as moral philosophers proclaim, they should be allowed to look for moral values in various places, including religious sources. D.Z. Phillips has alleged that philosophers are often reluctant to accept the heterogeneity of moral values.[8] Some secular moral philosophers are hesitant to accept religion as a source of moral values, a possible exemplification of the "secular humanism" that some American religious groups decry. Nevertheless, it is a fact that many Americans derive most of their moral values from their religious faith. For countless Americans, says Os Guiness, a British social scientist, their commitment to a public philosophy or the common good is rooted in their religious beliefs.[9] It is interesting to note that Lawrence Kohlberg, after many years of promoting a six-stage theory of moral development, has recently added a seventh stage, which is religious. A political scientist, Kent Greenawalt, has contended that if people must draw from their personal experiences and commitments to some degree, people with religious experiences and convictions, and the moral insights those convictions provide, should not be denied the opportunity to embrace them.[10] The first amendment to the United States Constitution allows people to base their values on their religious faith, a crucial part of religious freedom. Stephen Carter's book *The Culture of Disbelief* develops a strong case for allowing religious beliefs and the values that accompany them to receive a more prominent hearing than they generally get in contemporary America.[11]

Historical Precedence

The claim that religious ethics preceded philosophical ethics has been advanced. In his guidebook on ethics, Peter Singer treated the ethical traditions of the world religions before discussing Western philosophical ethics. James F. Drane says that before the historical development of secularization within Western history, virtually every moral system had its roots in religion. Drane further contends that during the Middle Ages natural law theory as posited by Aquinas reduced the influence of religion on morality, and that with the Enlightenment, and Kant in particular, the independence of morality from religion took root. This independence is now accepted by most Western intellectuals.[12] Persons favoring a relationship between religion and morality would like to return to the past.

Morality Can Lead to Religion

It is possible, as shown above, to speak of the historical precedence of religion. Conversely, however, circumstances can be found where moral aspirations and actions can lead to religion. Individuals can set very high moral standards for themselves and not be able to reach them. To paraphrase Browning, our reach may exceed our grasp. Drane states the point succinctly: "When ethics runs us against its own limits, it opens into another reality—the religious reality."[13] Humans who strive after the excellence in moral virtues that Aristotle advocated often despair of achieving them—they need additional resources. And these resources are frequently found in religion. A Japanese philosopher, Kitaro Nishida, argues that those who try to think seriously about how they should live cannot help but feel an intense religious demand.[14] It has also been observed that in order to practice the Christian virtue of love, we need the energy that enables us to love each other. And this energy is found in transcendent reality.

Kant's moral philosophy, which regarded religion as a product of moral consciousness, reinforces this idea. Kant realized that in order to faithfully fulfill the duties that rational moral laws placed on them, persons had to believe that their moral efforts were not in vain, that their efforts would be rewarded. For this to be possible, Kant had to "postulate" an antecedent moral order, the existence of God and immortality. The philosopher who so wanted to separate religion and morality actually ended up making them practically inseparable!

Religion as a Ground for Morality

The question of finding an adequate justification for our deepest moral beliefs was pursued at some length in the previous chapter. The difficulties of making reason and/or science the primary ground of moral values were noted. The claim here is that religion is able to provide an adequate ground for morality, and that religious beliefs help answer the profound question of why I should be moral.

How does religion answer this question? In two books, *Religious Reason: The Rational and Moral Basis of Religious Belief* and *Religion and Moral Reason*, Ronald M. Green argues that the "deep structures" of religion contain three essential elements: a method of moral reasoning involving "the moral point of view," a set of beliefs affirming the reality of moral retribution, and a series of transmoral beliefs that suspend moral judgment and retribution when that is needed to overcome moral paralysis and despair.[15] All three furnish a ground for religious morality, but the one that speaks of retribution may be most convincing, because it provides rational and emotional reasons for being moral. Alvin Plantinga and George

Mavrodes contend that unbelievers have no rational basis for being moral. Just feeling an obligation will not move one to action. Without God, Plantinga and Mavrodes believe, morality is odd at best and stupid at worst.[16]

Morality that springs from religion has its ground in myth and story, a truth that John F. Haught captures: "What grounds morality is a fundamental vision about reality as such. The mythic conception of reality has primacy over moral aspirations and provides its foundations. But even more important (to stay with the Biblical example) the necessary prerequisite of vigorous moral commitments that express faithfulness, love and trust in our relations with others is the acceptance by faith that reality as a matter of objective fact is grounded in a divine promise of fidelity. Without a conviction that the religious vision is true, religious morality is inert. Without a belief that the vision bears relation to what is *really* the case, there can be no ethical enthusiasm."[17]

The anthropologist Bronislaw Malinowski has observed that myths help to support morality. Rollo May goes so far as to declare that without myths there will be no morality.

What makes religion a satisfactory ground of morality? Religious philosophers/theologians give similar answers. They argue that without religious faith, life, the universe, and moral actions lack meaning. Louis Pojman believes that without an acceptance of God as Creator/Parent, it becomes difficult to say just why the basic moral belief that humans have worth makes sense.[18] James Gustafson maintains that the question of why we should be moral is not answered satisfactorily by ethical reasoning alone, for it is a question that refers to fundamental commitments. Moral answers are often influenced by religious or postethical perspectives.[19] A religious worldview may be necessary, William Frankena acknowledges, to show that we should be moral and do what is virtuous, right, and good in the first place. Religion gives morality a transcendent base. Bertrand Russell, an avowed atheist, once said: "I cannot see how to refute the arguments for the subjectivity of ethical values, but I find myself incapable of believing that all that is wrong with war and cruelty is that I don't like it." Although he found it impossible to believe in God, Russell may have yearned for a morality having a transcendent source.

In *A History of God,* Karen Armstrong alludes to Max Horkheimer, a German social theorist of the Frankfurt school, who regarded "God" as an important idea. Horkheimer said that whether we believe in God or not, and whether God exists or not, is superfluous. Without the idea of God there is no absolute meaning, truth, or morality, and ethics becomes simply a matter of taste, mood, or whim. Armstrong alleges that, for Horkheimer, "unless politics and morality somehow include the idea of 'God,' they will remain pragmatic and shrewd rather than wise. If there is no absolute, there is no reason that we should not hate or that war is worse than peace."[20]

In a similar vein, Hans Küng quotes words from Freud: "When I ask myself why I have always behaved honorably, ready to spare others and be kind whenever possible, and why I did not give up doing so when I observed that in that way one harms oneself and becomes an anvil because other people are brutal and untrustworthy, then, it is true, I have no answer."[21]

Religion Influences
and Shapes Culture

Does religion shape culture, or does culture shape religion? The most reasonable response to this kind of question is that they actually shape each other. Religions, along with their moral ideals, become embedded in culture. Judaism and Christianity are deeply embedded in Western culture, as Confucianism and Taoism are in Chinese culture, as Hinduism is in Indian culture, and so forth. Larry Shinn notes that because social mores and customs are bound up with religious beliefs, the distinction between cultural and religious norms is not always distinct. Social and political documents, such as the United States Constitution, contain a mingling of religious and social ideas.[22] Cultural values can stem from religious, as well as other, sources. The widely accepted cultural view that all life is valuable probably comes from the religious teaching that all of life comes from God and therefore has value.

That Western culture is now going through a process of secularization is generally recognized. Religious beliefs once tremendously important in Western societies are now much less so. However, the process of secularization has not entirely detracted from the capacity of many Americans to envision their lives as in some sense participating in a sacred reality. It is true that some people today are unable, for various reasons, to so participate. The German philosopher Jürgen Habermas has commented: "So, I do not believe that we as Europeans can seriously understand concepts like morality and ethics, personality and individuality, freedom and emancipation . . . without appropriating for ourselves the substance of a salvation-historical thought which originated in Judaism and Christianity."[23] Basil Mitchell agrees, for he argues that the Western moral and philosophical tradition has been significantly influenced by Christian conceptions of the nature and predicament of humans, and that it is highly doubtful that the intuitions of a traditional conscience (one still influenced by religious views) can be defended in terms of an entirely secular worldview.[24] A continuing reciprocal influence between religion and culture can be expected.

Religion and Autonomy

Western religions have been roundly criticized for being authoritarian and restrictive of human freedom and autonomy. Kant saw Judaism and Christianity, with their emphasis on obeying God's will, as an infringement on human autonomy. His criticisms have some validity, but the record is ambiguous. Religions are not always as rigid as thought; there may actually be more room for flexibility in religious ethics than there is in Kantian ethics.

A brief look at how religious people make moral decisions shows that religions allow more freedom than is often recognized. People of faith, particularly those belonging to Western religions, seek to know the will and purpose of God, that being or force who is good without qualification. This knowledge is sought in various ways: prayer, meditation, and worship; careful reading and study of the scriptures of one's religion; serious reflections on the writings and teachings of one's tradition; exercising reason about what is right and good and virtuous; thinking about human needs and how they can best be met; seeking the counsel of religious leaders; using moral principles like nonmaleficence and beneficence and trying to find the best ways for applying these principles to real life situations; and so forth. These different approaches to making moral judgments and decisions encourage freedom and autonomy.

A philosophical theory often discussed within philosophical ethics called the divine command theory has been severely attacked by moral philosophers as degrading to human dignity and freedom. The theory affirms that moral decisions are best made by finding out what God commands, as these dictates have been revealed by God to certain persons (e.g., the Ten Commandments, revealed to Moses). On the surface, this theory seems to suggest that humans have no freedom, but that as creatures of God's making they should meekly obey whatever God commands. When so interpreted, human freedom is negated.

There are valid criticisms of this theory, but the deficiency of the above criticism is that it focuses on one side of God's nature as portrayed by the biblical writers—the side connected with law and judgment. Several biblical writers, however, both Jewish and Christian, point to a God of love, mercy, and compassion, a God who will not force God's will on anyone. It is not fair to Western religious traditions as a whole to emphasize only one side of the ways in which God is depicted in these traditions. Furthermore, there are recent cogent defenses of the divine command theory that definitely retain human freedom. Christian ethicists have consistently emphasized human freedom and dignity.

This seems like an appropriate place to deal with the assertion that religious believers do not always act in morally commendable ways, and

that unbelievers may at times be more moral in their behavior than believers. This observation has merit and is probably empirically provable.
But in order to demonstrate it, agreement on what moral behavior is, and
just who is a religious believer and unbeliever, is necessary. Assuming
such agreement possible, I suspect that considerable evidence will be
found to support the claim that believers are not always moral and unbelievers are sometimes very moral. This is understandable because, as
just discussed, religious morality does not negate human freedom. Believers are free to follow or not follow the moral ideals of their religious
traditions. Believers are also quite fallible in their understanding of just
what constitute God's commands. Many religious believers readily admit that they cannot be absolutely sure what God wills, and that seeking
to know God's purposes is an activity prone to error. If religious faith allows autonomy, it must allow for mistakes. Incidentally, the same religious traditions that allow human freedom also recognize the reality of
sin and evil.

Religion and Guilt

Another criticism of religious morality is that it causes guilt feelings
within believers. Since it is extremely difficult, if not impossible, to per-
fectly follow the moral ideals of a given religion, those who try to do so
will inevitably come to feel very guilty about not being able to do so. Guilt
feelings can become a very heavy burden and engender psychological disorders. Freud strongly criticized the guilt-producing features of religion.
The fact that the moral ideals of a religion and the inability to completely
attain them can lead to an unhealthy guilt should be recognized.

As usual, there is another side. It is not fair to say that religion simply
makes people feel guilty, for religions also offer grace and forgiveness. We
have seen Ronald Green's proposal that the "deep structures" of religion
contain three essential elements, the third being a series of transmoral beliefs that suspend judgment and retribution when that is needed to overcome paralysis and despair. Green is referring to the religious doctrine of
grace, which to a greater or lesser extent is found within all religions. Grace
points to God's unconditional love, freely bestowed on all, whether de-
served or not. God's love does not have to be earned. Like human love at
its best, God's love is freely given to persons who desire it and in faith accept it. People of faith who are not able to keep all, or even most, of the
moral ideals embraced and taught by their religion need not wallow in
guilt. Paul Tillich wrote about overcoming a "graceless moralism," and
Lewis Smedes expressed the same idea by saying that "being forgiven is
more important than being right."[25]

Religion and Morality
Share an Essence

In his book *Morality and Beyond,* Paul Tillich supports the inseparability of religion and morality by arguing that "morality is intrinsically religious and religion is intrinsically ethical," and that "neither is dependent on the other, and neither can be substituted for the other." In tightly argued chapters, Tillich deals with the religious element of the moral imperative, the religious source of the moral demand, and the religious element in moral motivation. The moral imperative, according to Tillich, is a command to become what one potentially is—a person within a community of persons. The unconditional character of this moral imperative gives ultimate seriousness to both culture and religion. The will of God is thus not an external will or an arbitrary law imposed on us by a heavenly tyrant, but our essential being in all its potentialities. Religion as a state of being grasped by an ultimate concern or by something one takes unconditionally seriously leads to the religious dimension within the moral imperative. If the religious element is intrinsic to the moral imperative, conflict between secular and religious ethics (or between reason- and faith-determined ethics) is unnecessary.[26] In succeeding chapters, Tillich shows the religious dimension of the moral demand and moral motivation in ways that substantiate his central thesis, that religion and morality are virtually inseparable. Very few secular thinkers will entertain, let alone agree, with Tillich, but his ideas deserve consideration.

Inseparability Is
Philosophically Defensible

A recent book by a University of Chicago philosopher and theologian, Franklin I. Gamwell, entitled *The Divine Good: Modern Moral Theory and the Necessity of God,* provides a cogent defense of the inseparability of religion and morality. His underlying thesis is that the validity of moral claims presupposes the existence of God, and that one cannot affirm or deny any moral claim without implicitly affirming a divine reality. Gamwell says: "If one means by 'God' a being or an individual that is the source and end of all things, theism includes the conviction that God alone provides the authentic *telos* for the human enterprise as such. In other words, a divine reality is one upon which all worth or importance depends. It follows that adherents of theistic religions compromise the integrity of their religious beliefs insofar as they believe that a secularistic morality is possible. To believe in God and also to affirm a common morality that is neither explicitly nor implicitly theistic is to embrace an inconsistent self-understanding. For the same reason, theistic belief cannot consistently endorse the view that religious associations have no importance to the process by which the character and activities of the public order are defined. It is appropriate to say, then, that the argument here is an attempt to reassert and redeem the integrity of religious convictions in modern life."

Among the major points Gamwell makes in defending his thesis, the following are notable: (1) Autonomy and rationality, two emphases of modernity, are needed. (2) The best features of Aristotle and Kant should be kept. (3) The Aristotelian notion that the good life is one directed to a good end (the teleological) is very important. (4) Kant is correct in seeing moral claims as a priori and transcendental in nature. (5) Aristotle's teleological ethics and Kant's transcendental ethics cannot be sustained without theism. (6) The end that is good without qualification is the divine reality; God is the source and end of everything. (7) Neoclassical theism (as in Charles Hartshorne) is preferable to the classical theism that Kant severely damaged. Gamwell realizes that the theistic claim is metaphysical and argues that theism is philosophically defensible.[27]

Secular philosophers who read Gamwell will have criticisms, but it seems to me that he is correct. As a person of religious faith, I find it impossible to separate my religious self and my moral self, even though I have observed that, for some persons religion and morality are quite separable. In arguing that, for a genuine theist, religion and morality are inseparable, Gamwell is right. This does leave us, however, with the huge question of how theists should relate to the many nontheists in modern societies.

Moral Codes Are Accepted by Faith

If it is true that moral codes are accepted by faith, secular morality can have religious overtones. Faith here is not religious faith, but simply believing in what cannot be proved. A Jewish thinker, Irving Kristol, has observed that every moral code, including that of secular humanism, is accepted by faith.[28] Because our reason for being a moral person relates to our "basic commitments," Gustafson affirms that moral life includes faith and beliefs.

After several years of teaching philosophical ethics, I have concluded that a measure of faith is an essential element in being moral, and have so argued with friends, students, and colleagues who adopt a secular approach to morality. At the very least, in order to know and do what is right and good, I have to believe that this is what I ought to do. In order to treat others kindly and lovingly, I have to believe that I ought to be such a person. To truly practice honesty, compassion, and other virtues, I have to believe that these qualities are real and of value. I also need faith in my capacity, perhaps with a little help, to embody them. Morality requires faith. If this is true, then moral acts may not be entirely separate from religious faith.

Religion Supports Morality

In a book entitled *Morality: A New Justification of the Moral Rules,* Bernard Gert points out the difference between religion's supporting morality in general, and religion's supporting its own particular moral rules and ideals.[29] This suggests another reason for claiming that religion and morality are practically inseparable. One expects a given religion to promote and practice its own moral ideals. A serious participant in a religious tradition will regard all dimensions of that tradition as a whole greater than the sum of its parts. For people of religious faith, whatever that faith may be, religion and morality tend to be inseparable.

But if religion not only supports the morality of its own tradition, but supports morality in general, we have another example of the inseparability of religion and morality. Is it true that religion supports morality in general, even morality that does not have an explicit or implicit religious source? I believe so, for I have observed that Christians are often very sympathetic to moral values from outside their particular tradition. When the Catholic bishops of the United States wrote encyclicals on subjects of peace and economic justice, they drew on secular moral views as well as the moral teachings of their own faith community. Liberal Protestants have often been open (some would say too open) to secular moral philosophy, frequently adopting the language of secular moral philosophy. The willingness of religious ethics to accept insights from secular insights (and vice versa) seems commendable, for this kind of reciprocity makes a common morality possible—the public philosophy and civic public square that the Williamsburg Charter recommends.

Concluding Comments

Before furnishing several quotes that support the option of inseparability, I wish to acknowledge that many of the arguments of this chapter are debatable. I do not fully subscribe to all of them, but I have sought to present as strong a case as possible for the option of inseparability. And I will try to do the same for the remaining options.

However, even if some of the above arguments are not entirely plausible, they reinforce the position that religion and morality are too close to completely separate. In this way, these arguments add to the relational option, which will be considered after discussing the arguments for a definite separation of religion and morality.

While investigating this subject, I found it interesting that several notable people have spoken eloquently about the need for a close relation between religion and morality:

The attempts to found a morality apart from religion are like the attempts of children, who, wishing to transplant a flower that pleases them, pluck it from the roots that seem to them unpleasing and superfluous, and stick it rootless into the ground. Without religion there can be no real, sincere morality, just as without roots there can be no real flower.

—Leo Tolstoy

If God does not exist, all things are permissible.

—Spoken by Ivan, in *The Brothers Karamazov*,
Fyodor Dostoyevsky

Of all the dispositions and habits which lead to political prosperity, religion and morality are indispensable supports. . . . And let us with caution indulge the supposition that morality can be maintained without religion. . . . Reason and experience both forbid us to expect that national morality can prevail in exclusion of religious principle.

—George Washington, Farewell Address

We have no government armed with power capable of contending with human passions unbridled by morality and religion. Our constitution was made only for a moral and a religious people. It is wholly inadequate to the government of any other.

—John Adams

To suppose that any form of government will secure liberty or happiness without any form of virtue in the people is a chimerical idea.

—James Madison

Our government makes no sense unless it is founded on a deeply held religious faith, and I don't care what it is.

—Dwight Eisenhower

[It] is only in . . . faith that sees beyond the here and now, that we find the rationale for our daring notions about the inalienable rights of free men and women. . . . The Western ideas of freedom and democracy spring directly from the Judeo-Christian religious experience.

—Ronald Reagan

We also say that the moral values that religion generated and embodied for centuries can help in the work of renewal in our country, too.

—Mikhail Gorbachev

Chapter 5

Religion and Morality Are Separable

The second option for the encounter of religion and morality calls for making them totally or partly separable. Naturally, the persuasiveness of the arguments for separation somewhat diminish the arguments for inseparability. With this possibility in mind, we now consider several pertinent reasons for keeping religion and morality separate and different activities.

There Is More to Religion than Morality

Morality as a viable dimension of religion has been described, and claims for both a religious and a philosophical ethics have been proposed. If these claims are valid, the separation of religion and morality is not a denial of the possibility of a religious contribution to morality. Religion can still be seen as one of the sources of morality. Only secularists who tend to transform secularism into a religion will disagree.

Nevertheless, religion should not be reduced to morality. Enlightenment thought veered in this direction. Beginning with Kant, who made morality the very essence of religion and relegated positive religious convictions to a secondary place, Enlightenment figures virtually ignored religious experience. The religious preference of that time, which came to be called deism, reduced religion to moral beliefs and practices. Ronald Green alleges that because of this Enlightenment reduction of religion to morality, Romantic figures like Schleiermacher and Otto sought to develop a place for religion independent of its ethical significance.[1]

For people actively involved in it, religion is a lot more than morality. The dimension of worship or ritual found within religions is an example of this truth. In worship, a relationship with a worthy Reality is experienced. This kind of experience is not moral in nature, but a religious experience. Robin Gill declares that moral values are not the reason for the existence of the Christian religion; the value system is secondary to the worldview.[2] An expression of this view goes back to my youth, as I heard elders in my religious community say that being a moral person is not the same as being a Christian. The same could be said of being a Jew, a Muslim, or whatever. Rudolph Otto argued that a relation to the divine can be ultimately independent of moral considerations. The numinous overrides the moral as ground and source.[3] Religion is not a means to the end of morality, for religion can be an end in itself. Religion is much more than a commitment to ethical behavior. Edward Long Jr. has noted that scholars of comparative religion frequently compare religion without calling much attention to morality—other aspects of religion are accorded greater importance.[4] The function of religion is not to make people morally good (even if this is the result), but to provide transcendence and meaning. Morality may be the fruit of religion, but morality is not the reason people practice religion. The Danish philosopher Kierkegaard believed that humans go through three states—the aesthetic, the ethical, and the religious. The stages can be interwoven, but for Kierkegaard the religious stage definitely differed from the ethical.

Nonreligious People Can Be Moral

A reason often cited for separating religion and morality is this: People who are not religious can be and often are quite moral. Is this popular notion true? An adequate answer depends on how one defines and describes both religion and morality. If religion includes the seven dimensions described in chapter 1, particularly religion as an act of valuing and religion as a yearning for self-transformation, it becomes difficult to imagine a morality not directly or indirectly connected to religion, or a morality that has absolutely no religious overtones or connotations. Moreover, if the acceptance of a moral code implies a kind of faith, the popular understanding of the total separation of religion and morality can at least be questioned.

However, if we reverse the statement and say that religious people can be immoral, we begin to realize that religion and morality are not automatically connected. We can readily agree that religious people ought to be moral rather than immoral people. But it is obvious that people who consider themselves religious, and are so considered by others, sometimes act immorally. Regrettably, avowedly religious people have participated to some extent in such morally dastardly events as the Crusades, the Inquisition, the Holocaust, and the killing of physicians who perform abortions. The fact that religious people do not always live morally exemplary lives makes it difficult to maintain the position of the total inseparability of religion and morality.

More specificity about what is meant by not religious in this context may help. The term has largely to do with self-designation, as seen in statements like "I am not a religious person" or "I am a religious person." It relates to how one refers to oneself: as a theist, an atheist, an agnostic, or a humanist. The latter term is more problematic, because there are religious as well as secular humanists. A theist believes that God exists, an atheist believes that God does not exist. An agnostic says it cannot be known whether God exists or not. Humanists tend to deny the existence of a transcendent reality (which seems to make them atheists), or at least to argue that the quality of human life right now is much more important than speculating over the existence of unprovable realities (a view that seems to make them agnostic). Matters of religious belief can be fairly complex.

Our question remains: Can people who claim to be atheist or agnostic be moral in their actions? It seems to me that people who so label themselves not only can, but often do act in morally commendable ways. I have observed atheists, agnostics, and humanists demonstrate compassion and justice; their moral beliefs motivated them to become active participants in peace, justice, and environmental movements. If these movements are moral in nature, as most will acknowledge, then nonreligious persons can be moral. One well-known atheist, Ludwig Feuerbach, put it this way: "In annulling what is above man theologically, atheism does not annul what is ethically and naturally higher; the ethically higher is the ideal every man must pursue if he is to make anything worthwhile of himself, but the ideal must be a human ideal and aim."[5]

Further examples confirm this thesis. A study by Samuel and Pearl Oliner of European people who helped Jews escape the Holocaust provides a dramatic illustration. Assisting Jews in this way required courage and compassion. The Oliners discovered that many of the people who helped Jews at this time were not overtly religious; they were not active members of a religious group. Though they were not particularly religious, most observers will freely call them moral persons.[6]

The American scientist and writer Isaac Asimov declared that even if people do not believe in God they can have strong feelings about right and wrong.[7] This conviction is confirmed by the fact that in times of compulsory military service the Supreme Court of the United States has not required people requesting conscientious objector status (opposition to service in the armed forces) to believe in God.

In American society, large numbers of people respond to calls for helping others in need without pointing to overt religious reasons for so acting. Artists, writers, musicians, filmmakers, and others who ostensibly embrace no religious faith are often deeply concerned about peace, justice, and environmental issues. Augustine once commented that even nonbelievers can recognize the deep tendency of human beings to moral evil. People able to recognize evil can also identify and, at least to some extent, strive to do the good.

There are numerous additional reasons for claiming that nonreligious people can act morally.

First, religion is one of the sources of moral beliefs and values, but not the only one. Gustafson considers it very arbitrary to insist that all moral ideas come from religion. Numerous diverse sources of moral beliefs abound. One of the largest is society and culture itself. There are moral communities that owe little to religion. Moral ideas are practically omnipresent, almost impossible to avoid. Mary Midgley comments that moral language is like the air we breathe.[8] Moral ideas from our society shape our attitudes and behavior. We often acquire moral beliefs from parents and friends. At times, we discover moral values in science and philosophy. Art is another source of moral values, especially literature. Robert Coles has nicely shown that stories of morally exemplary people are fruitful in teaching moral values. And there are naturalists who see patterns and structures for moral living in nature itself. Thomas Jefferson actually talked about living according to the laws of nature. If it is true that the influence of the Judeo-Christian tradition is slipping, we can be grateful that other sources of moral values exist.

Second, there is the role of conscience, usually defined as an inner sense of right and wrong, good and evil. This concept is exceedingly controversial. Most moral scientists contend that it is simply the voice of parents and society. Even so, conscience makes it possible to call attention to the self as a moral agent. H. Richard Niebuhr was a Christian ethicist who emphasized being responsible and using discernment and moral intuition.[9] If conscience is something all humans possess in some measure, the fact that nonreligious people can be moral is understandable.

Third, the fact that people can have many different reasons for acting the way they do seems apparent. Robert Adams has called attention to the "plurality of motives" for human actions.[10] There are religious motives for acting morally, and nonreligious motives for acting morally. A person can help another human being simply because he believes it is the right or good thing to do.

Fourth, there is a little-used Christian doctrine called "common grace," which affirms that persons who are not Christians, and who have not experienced what Christians call the new birth, can perform noble deeds because God's grace is working in their lives, even if they do not realize it. Diogenes Allen says that an agnostic may receive God's grace unknowingly, and Christians may have been deeper into evil than some agnostics were before they changed direction.[11] This doctrine will not appeal to secular people, but it can help religious people accept the fact that nonreligious people can be moral.

Fifth, many religious people willingly concede that those without religious faith can lead an authentically human and moral life. Hans Küng embraces this position and forthrightly declares that humans as rational beings have an autonomy that enables them to have a basic trust in reality. Küng believes that humanists are capable of living a humane ethic.

Sixth, another Jewish-Christian belief is that God can use nonreligious people or unbelievers to accomplish God's purposes. Robert McAfee Brown points to a teaching within the Hebrew Bible that declares that God used the Assyrians, pagan neighbors of the Hebrews, to fulfill God's plan for the Hebrews. Brown applies this idea to modern nonreligious writers who are able to express deep religious and moral truths in their writings. He calls them "Assyrians in modern dress."[12]

Seventh, people can be influenced by religious belief without realizing it. The influence of religious teachings may be indirect. Religious views often become secularized and part of general social thinking. For example, the religious teaching prohibiting the taking of life becomes a precept of respect for others or reverence for life. It can be difficult to distinguish the religious and nonreligious elements in a given moral position. As religious views become secularized, the religious background of a moral belief fades away and the religious origins of the belief are essentially forgotten. Nonreligious people may be moral because they are acting out religious moral beliefs that have become accepted by society as a whole.

Lastly, nonreligious people can be moral by keeping religious or divine commands simply because they want to do so, and in the process may or may not come to faith in the God behind these commands. Abraham Joshua Heschel spoke of following *mitzvah* (religious commands/laws) as an "antecedent of faith."[13] Thus, one can be moral without having a religious faith, but in being moral may actually be moving toward religious faith.

Historical Support for Separation

Christian ethicists have often argued that it was only after the Enlightenment of the seventeenth and eighteenth centuries that Western culture separated religion and morality. However, in both ancient and medieval periods there existed those who believed that religion and morality should be disconnected.

In the ancient period, both Greeks and Romans viewed religion and morality as different activities. The Greek and Latin origins of the words "ethics" and "morality" indicated no mention of religion because of this separateness. Socrates, Plato, and Aristotle, the most influential of the Greek philosophers, definitely separated religion and morality. For Socrates, moral philosophy was a matter of wisely answering the basic question of how should one live.

For Plato, morality was independent of religion as well as the judge of religion. In the dialogue called *Euthyphro,* we hear Socrates asking the famous question of whether something is holy (or right or good) because God commands it, or whether God commands something simply because it is holy, right, or good in itself. This statement is subject to interpretation, but it is generally agreed that for Plato something was right and good in itself and not right and good because God commanded it. Plato wanted his fellow Greeks to think deeply about right and good in itself, as ideas or forms, and thus to go beyond what the gods commanded. The fact that the Greek gods were sometimes not good role models may have influenced Plato's ideas on this subject.

Aristotle also saw morality and ethics as separate from religion. He believed that people act purposefully, with an end in view, pursuing the moral virtues that lead to happiness. So the Greek philosophers, if not the common people, desired to keep religion and morality separate.

During the Middle Ages, Thomas Aquinas became the prime example of one who sought to separate religion and morality, despite the fact that he was a Christian theologian. In espousing natural law theory, Aquinas went back to Aristotle. This theory, as noted earlier, contends that by employing reason, without religion or revelation, one can understand what is right and good. For Aquinas, actions are prohibited or encouraged because they are evil or good in themselves. James Rachels actually argues that Aquinas denied divine command theory and associated morality with reason rather than religion. This may be Rachel's reading of Aquinas, but it is doubtful that Aquinas, as a Dominican priest, wanted to completely divorce morality from religion. That he was willing to partially separate them is correct, but for Aquinas natural law was grounded in God, and therefore morality derived from natural law is still at least somewhat dependent on God.

With the European Enlightenment and the beginning of modernity, the drive to separate religion and morality flourished. As noted, Kant was a dominant figure in this movement, but at the same time and a little later figures such as David Hume, Jeremy Bentham, and John Stuart Mill pushed hard for the independence of morality from religion. It was Mill who said that it is possible to take the morality of a religion and leave the religion behind.[14]

Contemporary philosophical thought definitely views religion and morality as separate. Following in the train of Aristotle, Kant, and Mill, contemporary moral philosophers see religion and morality as independent. Analytic philosophy is one example of this outlook. Richard Brandt, a representative of this school, argues that since God's existence cannot be proved, theological propositions cannot justify ethical principles. One cannot derive ethical conclusions from statements containing no ethical terms. Logic allows no inferences of this type.[15] A philosophical defense of morality appeals to what in principle is available to all human beings, whatever their religious beliefs. Historical support for separating religion and morality is substantial.

Religion and Morality Involve Different Activities

This reason for making religion and morality separate gets to the heart of the matter. It recognizes that religion and morality can be related in meaningful ways, but strongly suggests that religion and morality can be differentiated. Among some differences between religion and morality, the following can be noted:

Religion and morality involve different *attitudes.* Morality focuses primarily on behavior, or an inner realization that we are responsible for our actions. The attitude of religion, on the other hand, embodies attitudes of awe and reverence toward that which is transcendent and sacred. Kierkegaard used Socrates and Jesus as examples of the ethical and religious: Socrates looked for truth from within, Jesus looked for truth from without, from God. Or, as James Drane puts it, Socrates before the Athenian court exemplifies morality, but Jesus' attitude and disposition toward death illustrates religion.[16]

Religion and morality also differ in *actions and duties.* Perhaps one of the best illustrations of this comes from the Ten Commandments of the Hebrew Bible (Exodus 20). The first four commandments give religious duties: no other gods, no images of God, no profane use of God's name, and observance of the Sabbath. The last six give moral duties: honoring parents, no killing, and no adultery, stealing, false witnessing, or coveting. Religious duties are not moral duties, and vice versa. Religious duties focus on pleasing God; moral actions center on doing what is right and good to others. Religious duties require prayer and devotion; moral duties call for fulfilling responsibilities to fellow humans. Moral actions are directed toward affairs of an earthly life; religious actions are directed both to earthly affairs and also toward life beyond earthly existence.

The *training* involved is another way in which religion and morality are different. Religious training emphasizes a life of faith and relationship with God. Moral training emphasizes doing what is right and good.

Gustafson properly notes that moral training does not require religious training, and religious training does not necessarily lead to commendable conduct.

Another difference is that of *primary motivations and intentions* for actions. The reason for acting morally can be that of doing God's will or doing what is right out of love for God (religion), or that of doing one's duties and being responsible (morality). One can do what is right and good because one fears God's wrath if one fails to comply (religion); one can do what is right and good out of sincere concern and compassion for others (morality).

In what they *advocate and teach*, religion and morality are different. A comparison of religious and philosophical ethics illustrates this point. Religious ethics often conflicts with modern secular philosophical ethics. An area in which this is evident is sexual ethics. Religious ethics usually takes a negative view of premarital sex, adultery, abortion, and homosexual relations, whereas modern philosophical ethics is generally more accepting of these practices. Further, religious ethics tends to favor capital punishment, while philosophical ethics usually argues against it. In many ways the differences between religious and moral activity are observable.

Religion Favors a Separation

That moral philosophy favors a separation between religion and morality is not surprising. The idea that religion also may favor a separation may seem strange, but some representatives of religion believe that a separation between religion and morality is desirable. Why do they so believe?

One answer is that separation can be wholesome. A respectful distance between persons has benefits; it allows each person to be himself or herself. Even in a united, close-knit community, the kind of separation that permits individuals the freedom to be the unique selves they are is valuable.

Moreover, most religions do not teach that only religious people, or the people belonging to a certain religion, can be moral or have ethical insights. Many religious believers freely acknowledge that nonbelievers have strong moral beliefs that issue in morally commendable behavior. People with a religious identity, well rooted in a religious faith and community, often become open and receptive to religious and moral truths from varied sources.

Religious thinkers sometimes refer to the existence of necessary moral truths, which result from the way God has structured the world. There are moral truths whose truth does not depend on God's command. Rape is wrong, and not just because God says so; and compassion is right, not simply because God says so.

Moreover, as Bernard Gert proposes, since God gave rules other than moral rules (within the Judeo-Christian tradition), we need ways of distinguishing moral rules from nonmoral rules. Gert claims that the fact that God gave moral rules is not sufficient, for rules resting on revelation must be testable by reason. Religion is a source of moral beliefs, but religion alone does not determine what is moral.[17] Some religious ethicists will disagree with Gert, but his observation about differentiating between moral and nonmoral rules is helpful.

An unexpected example of this point comes from the work of Vincent McNamara, a Catholic ethicist who argues that many Catholic moral philosophers do not appeal to revelation. Instead, they see Christian morality as autonomous—they believe that morality can be the same for Christians and non-Christians, and that by reason (natural law theory) Christians can arrive at the same content as secular moral philosophers.[18] In the same vein, a moral philosopher from the Philosophy and Public Policy Center of the University of Maryland maintains that humans agree more on moral beliefs than on religious beliefs. His view suggests that moral judgments have a life of their own, whatever their long history, and that given the extent of religious conflict in the world, it is fortunate that this is so.[19]

A separation between religion and morality is closely related to the fact that religious and philosophical ethics are different. Chapters 2 and 3 described this difference. It may be largely one of reliance: philosophical ethics relies primarily on human reason, whereas religious ethics relies primarily on faith and revelation and only secondarily (yet significantly) on human reason.

Assistance and Similarities

A further reason for some measure of separation between religion and morality relates to the recognition of most religious ethicists of assistance from and similarities to secular moral philosophy. Gilbert Meilander has observed that Christian ethics, as one form of religious ethics, is both particular and general. The particular part refers to the specific moral values of the Christian tradition. The general part is that shared with other traditions, or with culture in general, which can be defended on grounds not peculiarly Christian.[20] Both Christian ethics and secular morality employ moral reasoning. Religious ethics often needs the philosophical vigor that secular philosophy provides. Robert Van Wyk points out that religious ethicists can be wrong and need correcting.[21] Even cherished religious beliefs and values can be, and often should be, modified. If religion is partly a matter of being open to all truth as God's truth, then religious morality ought to be willing to learn from moral philosophy. The opposite should also be true.

An allied point by Jacques Thiroux is that since religions frequently conflict with other religions, it is sometimes necessary to go outside of religion to find a mediator.[22] Moral philosophy can play this role. Of course, religions need not uncritically accept the views of moral philosophy, but there are times when philosophical ethics can nicely assist religious ethics. Religious people should be grateful for this possibility.

Religious observers are able to recognize similarities between religious and philosophical morality. As we've noted, there are times when religious ethics agrees with and supports secular ethics. This is not always so, of course, but one place where it seems to be true is the abortion issue. Moral philosophers are often antiabortion but pro-choice. It is also true that Protestant mainline denominations usually take the same approach, favoring abortion only for cases of rape, incest, and the health of the mother, while the same denominations actively advocate a woman's right and responsibility to choose in this matter. In this situation, it appears that religious and philosophical ethics are fairly close.

These statements are not contending that religious and philosophical ethics will always come out at the same place, for this is clearly not the case. Nevertheless, there are similarities. Chapter 7 contains a case study of one moral concern where religious and philosophical ethics have much in common. Of course, some Christian theologians and theologians of other religions have no interest in seeing similarities between religious and philosophical ethics. Some Christian ethicists continue to follow the pleading of Tertullian (a bishop of the early Christian church), who said, "What has Athens to do with Jerusalem?" Those who prefer to separate faith and reason are not likely to disappear.

Morality Can
Be Grounded—Without Religion

Another possible reason for separating religion and morality is connected to the conviction of moral philosophers that ethics be adequately grounded without resorting to religion. The complex issue of having sufficient reasons for our moral beliefs was discussed in chapter 3. Grounding beliefs relates to the larger question of knowledge itself: How do we *know* that our beliefs and statements are true? If all four of the traditional sources of knowledge (senses, reason, intuition, and authority) have validity, then moral insights that spring from these sources have a measure of justification. Edward Long Jr. provides an example of this process in showing how ethical judgments are developed: They begin with personal

experiences (in which one or more of the sources of knowledge are utilized), proceed to reflective generalizations, to social activity, and, finally,
to ethical pronouncements.[23] By following this process, or a similar one,
moral beliefs are grounded without relying on religion directly. For most
secular moralists, this type of grounding is sufficient.

Humanist philosophy furnishes an example. The *Humanist Manifesto I
& II* states that ethics is autonomous and situational, needing no ideological sanction.[24] Humanism favors a morality without religion. The situation
is somewhat complex, in that some humanists speak of secular humanism,
while others speak of humanism as a religion. Mary Midgley contends that
humanists who do not believe in God or a future life are in a stronger position to insist on making things better now, in this life: "If this is the only
life anybody has, then the fact that some people must spend it in such mis-
ery becomes more obviously and inexcusably scandalous. Salvation is
needed now; it cannot be put off to some vaguely planned future state."[25]
Her argument has merit, but one can still ask: "Why should I want to make
life better now?" The question as to why one should be moral remains
troublesome and pressing.

Morality Is Part of Human Nature

Morality is not only a dimension of religion; it is also a crucial part of
being human. Thoughtful persons have regarded morality as an aspect of
human nature that needs no particular relation to religion. Morality, they
will say, can stand on its own.

Integral to this understanding is the view that morality is rooted in self-
consciousness or reflection. Plato believed that humans are disposed toward thinking about the good. Humans ask themselves what they should
do—what is the right thing to do. Humans think about the kind of persons
they should be. Humans can visualize the consequences of their actions
and thereby decide to act a certain way. Midgley believes that thinking in
moral terms or categories is woven into the very fabric of our nature, and
that moral language is, as we noted, "like the air we breathe."[26] Thomas
Jefferson was sure that humans have an innate sense of right and wrong,
just by virtue of being human. James Q. Wilson agrees, and refers to the reality of a universal "moral sense" within humans.[27]

Natural law theory also supports the view that morality is part of human nature, for it contends that God has implanted natural or moral laws
within the faculty of human reason, thus providing rules for human conduct that come from human nature itself. The role of natural law theory
will be discussed further in the next chapter.

Similarly, there are those who root morality in psychology or biology.
Owen Flanagan, for instance, is sure that only through a credible picture

of human personality, or an accurate theory of human nature and agency via psychology, will we be able to develop realistic moral goals for human beings. We have noted that there are biologists who allege that morality is actually genetic, a product of evolution, in which everything, including moral behavior, has a material base. These biologists actually locate the source of morality in the program of the brain.[28] Psychology and biology thus locate the source of morality in human nature itself; no external source is needed.

Viewing morality as part of human nature makes credible Gustafson's view that the study of ethics should begin with a description and analysis of human nature. Differing perspectives on human nature will naturally affect the way we deal with morality.

Separation Is Necessary for Consensus

If humanity is ever to reach a moral consensus, or some kind of universal morality, a degree of separation or distance between religion and morality is necessary. Total separation is not required, but enough separation is needed to allow religion and morality to operate with the freedom that enables them to make their unique and respective contributions to a common morality.

Does our world need a common morality, a global ethic? Because of gigantic problems connected with ecological, economic, and ethnic disorders, I have concluded that a moral consensus among the world's people would be most helpful. It is highly doubtful that any of these problems, in their various manifestations, can be solved without a strong moral consensus. If this contention has any plausibility, it cannot be prudent to cut off people who have genuine concerns about moral issues simply because they have no real interest in religion. Nonreligious, secular people often have high moral ideals which they seek to embody in their style of living. For the sake of our planet, a genuine interactive dialogue between religious and nonreligious people about moral issues is imperative. We may pray to different gods, or to no gods, and still work together to revitalize our common life and enhance the common good. Robert Adams constructively notes that religious ethics can support the precepts of a common morality and add demands of its own.[29] And Os Guiness helpfully affirms that a common morality or a public philosophy rooted in religious beliefs is acceptable, because the public affirmations themselves are not religious.[30] A healthy separation of religion and morality should be conducive to the moral consensus we need.

Concluding Comments

Coming to the end of a chapter that has argued for a separation of religion and morality, and anticipating a chapter that will argue for a relationship between religion and morality, it might be constructive to express a view that at first may seem contradictory: a degree of separation between religion and morality is preferable to a total inseparability. Healthy relationships allow for freedom and autonomy, with sufficient distance for each party to remain who that party is. With this notion in mind, we turn to the central argument of this treatise—religion and morality are relational.

Chapter 6

Religion and Morality Are Relational

We have now come to the third way for religion and morality to deal with each other, the relational way. This option has both negative and positive implications: it affirms that religion and morality are neither virtually inseparable nor totally separable, but are relational. They have plenty to say to each other and should be in close contact with each other. A close conversation between religion and morality should be mutually beneficial. This conversation allows for the autonomy of both and encourages both to willingly accept each other. This way further implies that despite their legitimate differences, religion and morality can learn from and enrich each other. Relational is a rich word, suggesting interaction and reciprocity.

In the two preceding chapters, cases for inseparability and separability were developed. The task of this chapter is to build a case for relationality. This chapter is different from the past two in that its arguments constitute a proposal. They also express an underlying thesis and intentional conclusions. They are presented here in the spirit of an invitation to dialogue between those who primarily engage in philosophical ethics and those who mostly practice religious ethics.

Newer Understandings of Reality

An initial argument for a relational approach between religion and morality is that a relational approach corresponds with newer understandings of reality in general, as well as recent views about the reality of the universe and the self. It has now become fashionable among scientists and philosophers to discuss reality in terms of relatedness. Relationality thus describes the way it is, the way things are. According to Fritjof Capra, a physicist, viewing things within a framework of relationships is part of "new paradigm thinking" in science, which has shifted from the part to the whole, from structure to process, and from building to network as a metaphor for knowledge. New paradigm thinking in science is complemented by new paradigm thinking in theology and religion.[1]

Newer understandings of the universe (some will say it is rather ancient) place great emphasis on everything in the universe being related. Michael Talbot compares the universe to a hologram in which every portion is "infinitely connected" with every other portion.[2] The process philosophy of mathematician/philosopher Alfred North Whitehead (1861–1947), also called the philosophy of organism, is the source of much of this thinking. Whitehead contended that everything is interconnected yet intellectually separable, and that there is an organic relation within and between entities. Employing Whitehead's approach, John Haught comments: "Relationship, to speak somewhat paradoxically, turns out to be the very substance of things. Every entity is in some sense a synthesis of all the relations presented to it by its environment. There are no substances existing independently of relations. . . . Developments in science, especially evolutionary theory and modern physics, but increasingly other areas as well, have allowed us to view the universe in an increasingly organismic or relational way."[3]

Whitehead's process philosophy has influenced social scientists too. Sociologists David A. Fraser and Tony Campolo have commented that "the great chain of being" metaphor has been replaced by the notion of "a web of interconnections."[4] The image of the universe as dynamic and multicausal underlies the science of ecology and its organismic way of looking at the natural world. Of course, the debate over proper models and paradigms for understanding the natural order is ongoing. Sally McFague observes that many still prefer viewing the universe in a mechanical rather than an organic manner, seeing the world as a machine instead of as a body. The organic model supports both a radical individuality and differences, while insisting on the radical interdependence of all parts. McFague argues that "nothing is more central to the common creation story than the ancient and present character of mutual dependence of all life forms on one another and the life-supporting systems of our planet."[5]

In *The Death of Nature: Women, Ecology and the Scientific Revolution,* Carolyn Merchant writes eloquently about newer approaches to the universe and nature: "Along with current challenges to mechanistic teleology, holistic presuppositions about nature are being revived in ecology's premise that everything is connected to everything else and in its emphasis on the primacy of interactive processes in nature. All parts are dependent on one another and mutually affect each other and the whole."[6]

Newer understandings of the self also place the emphasis on relationality. W. H. Auden wrote that "no one exists alone," perhaps echoing John Donne's "No man is an island," or St. Paul's "We do not live to ourselves, and we do not die to ourselves" (Rom. 14:7). The self does not exist apart from relationships, for it is involved in a network of relationships, inter-connected with all of life. An individual is both separate and related, individual as well as social. Joseph H. Kupfer, in *Autonomy and Social Interaction*, maintains that autonomy and social interaction are reciprocal and significant for each other.[7] In the continuing emphasis on autonomy since the Enlightenment, this fact has been neglected by philosophers and psychologists. The three major schools of Western psychology—behaviorism, psychoanalysis, and humanistic psychology—regard the self as an isolated, lonely island. However, as John Bowlby in *Attachment and Loss* points out, it is only by engaging in interpersonal relationships that we begin to discover our uniqueness and individuality.[8] The fields of semiotics and structuralism also demonstrate that meaning is relational.

H. Richard Niebuhr developed an ethical theory in which relationality is a key concept. In *The Responsible Self*, Niebuhr referred to three types of ethics, in which the focus falls respectively on man the maker (*homo faber*), man the citizen (*homo politicus*), and man the responder (*homo dialogicus*). Teleological ethics emphasizes man the maker; deontological ethics, man the citizen; and the ethics of fittingness or responsibility, man the responder. We are persons in dialogue, who seek relationships with each other.[9] The self emerges in relation to others. Niebuhr's relational model has been noted by philosophical ethicists and is generally regarded as similar to the virtue ethics we have discussed.

If understandings of reality form a foundation for religion and morality (a defensible view), then these understandings of the universe and the self are of value beyond their support for religion and morality's being relational.

Beyond Derivation and Dependency

The second argument for religion and morality as relational is that this position enables us to go beyond seeing morality as derived from and dependent on religion, as well as seeing religion as derived from and dependent on morality. Religious ethicists have often argued for the first position, philosophical ethicists have frequently pushed the second.

Previously, I argued that making morality dependent on religion, or vice versa, is neither necessary nor fruitful. Making one dependent on or derived from the other ends up making one primary and the other secondary or, even worse, making one superior and the other inferior. This way ends in a relationship between religion and morality—a hostile one!

I am convinced that the arguments for separation in chapter 5 justify the conclusion that morality need not depend on religion. The claim that it must is not supportable because it is obvious that nonreligious people can be moral, and that religion and morality are distinguishable activities. Of course, it is one thing to claim that morality *must* be based on religion (not supportable), and another to claim that religion *may* deeply affect one's moral beliefs (very supportable). It is just as incorrect to say that all morality is dependent on religion as it is to say that no morality is dependent on religion.

Equally inappropriate is the claim that religion depends on or is derived from morality. Greek and Roman moral philosophy tended to make religion depend on morality. In *Euthyphro,* Socrates apparently preferred to call something good or holy because it is good and holy in itself, not because the gods declare it good or holy. Kant also preferred to begin with morality, the duties determined by reason that can lead to moral rules, despite the fact that he finally admitted the necessity of belief in God, freedom, and immortality as enforcers of rationally chosen rules. Since morality is only one dimension among others found within religion, making religion depend on morality is no more reasonable than making morality depend on religion.

The historical element is also relevant, for there have always been those who have argued for the historical precedence of religion as well as those who argue for the historical precedence of morality. For some religion came first, for others morality came first. In reality, it is doubtful that the historical precedence of either can be firmly established. Both religion and morality are ancient activities, a great part of being human. For a very long time humans have been making moral judgments about right and wrong, good and evil. And for a very long time humans have experienced the sacred and holy in the midst of their earthly existence. We cannot say with any certainty which one came first—nor do we need to.

The crucial point in this discussion is that neither religion nor morality is completely autonomous, without any dependencies and influences. Morality for the theist as well as the nontheist, the believer as well as the unbeliever, is not absolutely independent. Morality always has a social and cultural context. In *The Origins of Christian Morality,* Wayne A. Meeks substantiates his view that Christian morality was greatly influenced by its social and cultural setting. His comparisons of the moral views held by Christians with those of pagan philosophers reveal more similarities than differences.[10] Because religions have social and cultural contexts, none of the continuing religions of humanity can be understood apart from their cultural settings. Neither religion nor morality exists in splendid isolation!

Rather than point to one as dependent on or derived from the other, it is better to speak about the relationship of religion and morality and of how they continue to influence each other in mutually enriching ways. Healthy relationships, which allow for interaction and dialogue, are generally mutually rewarding.

Stanley Hauerwas has proposed that we cease talking about the relationship of religion and morality altogether and simply talk about the truth, whatever the source, religious or moral.[11] His proposal makes sense, because two such deep and serious human activities should not be totally separated. A healthy relationship is eminently desirable!

Beyond Inseparable and Separable

A relation between religion and morality makes possible the transcendence of two options we considered earlier—inseparability and separability. It does so by offering an attractive and appealing alternative, a more fruitful third option.

Such an alternative is necessary because the arguments for both inseparability and separability are not completely convincing. There are sound reasons for making religion and morality inseparable, as well as good arguments for keeping them separable. However, the good reasons given for one somewhat negate the sound reasons given for the other. Yet if the reasons advanced for both of them have any merit, it seems prudent to retain them to some degree rather than discard them completely.

A way out of this impasse is available through what many will call "a middle way," a way that establishes a balance through which the opposites are embraced. Relationality is this middle way, which makes it possible to go beyond the opposites of inseparation and separation.

The yin-yang concept of Chinese Taoism, along with Hegel's philosophy of history, nicely provide assistance for pursuing a balance between inseparable and separable and going beyond them. The yin-yang proposal affirms the complementarity of opposites, such as light and darkness, male and female, and so forth, and declares that a balance between opposites is helpful. It proposes that opposites actually need and complete each other. I believe that this Taoist approach is constructive.

The German philosopher Georg Wilhelm Hegel (1770–1831) proposed that history moves from thesis to antithesis to synthesis, with the synthesis subsequently becoming a new thesis. Hegel's scheme does not apply precisely, but we can roughly take the idea of religion and morality's being inseparable as a thesis, the idea of religion and morality's being separable as an antithesis, and the idea of religion and morality's being relational as a synthesis. Hegel saw the synthesis as capable of retaining the best parts of the thesis and antithesis; the thesis and antithesis are lifted up (the German verb he used was *aufheben*) and included within the synthesis.

An approach that enables us to go beyond inseparation and separation has these definite advantages:

—A relational approach helps us realize that while religion and morality are not necessarily related, they can be related. Many moral philosophers have insisted that there is no *necessary* relationship between religion and morality. This is correct, but it does not logically follow that there is no relationship. We should not argue a priori that they must be related (that they are inseparable), nor should we argue a priori that they cannot be related (that they are separable). Arguing for a possible relation is more plausible.

—It is often useful to go beyond one-sided views. Inseparable and separable represent one-sided views. We often want things to be black or white, one thing or the other, when in reality they may be gray, something in between. Also, if religion and morality are human activities, part of oneself, it makes little sense to totally separate these activities. Religion and morality are actually different activities of a single self.

—This approach fulfills one of the two basic human impulses for dealing with reality: that of integrating and reconciling things. The other impulse is that of taking things apart, fragmenting and deconstructing. The Greek words *symballein* (to throw together) and *diaballein* (to thrust apart) illustrate the two impulses. It is wise for humans to allow both impulses room for expression.

—The relational approach also enables us to realize, in Os Guiness's words, that "no truth, however clearly stated, is the whole truth. No single principle, however well applied, is the all-sufficient answer. All our truths, principles and emphases need balancing." George MacDonald also said it well: "Our human life is often, at best, but an oscillation between the extremes which together make the truth."[12] If this sounds a bit paradoxical, it is only because truth is often expressed in this way.

Reason in Perspective

The option of relationality enables us to put reason into a larger context. It does so by facilitating an awareness of the values and limitations of reason. Probably most philosophers recognize this double nature of reason. A relational approach makes possible a deep awareness of how both religious and nonreligious thinkers, believers and nonbelievers, deal with significant issues related to reason.

The values of reason are almost universally accepted by nonreligious and religious people. However, the word *reason* itself has various meanings in Western philosophical and religious thought. Reason can be described as the capacity for solving mathematical and practical problems, being able to draw logical conclusions. Tillich calls this "technical" reason. But reason can be much more. Plato saw reason as the faculty that enables humans to understand the eternal forms or ideas—truth, beauty, good (or goodness), freedom, equality, justice, and so forth. Many philosophers emphasize this form of reason, which Tillich calls "ontological" reason—"the structure of the mind which enables the mind to grasp and transform reality."[13] Humans use this form of reason in varying degrees; "ontological" reason is part of our common humanity, and is basic to the ethical theories we have discussed.

As one of the sources of knowledge and understanding, reason has been and will remain central in philosophical, religious, and moral thinking. Ronald Green maintains that reason has at least four forms: theoretical (what Tillich called ontological), prudential, moral, and religious. That religious teachers employ reason freely and fruitfully hardly needs mentioning. In the Buddhist tradition, wisdom precedes morality, as seen in the Eightfold Path. A Buddhist needs knowledge and wisdom in order to proceed to "right conduct." If wisdom is one of the higher forms of knowledge, the place of reason in religion is assured.

A further value of reason for both the religious and the nonreligious is its critical function. Reason helps us to make judgments, sort things out, and distinguish the wheat from the chaff. Reason enables us to identify true and false ideas, values, and beliefs. In this way, reason is the complement of faith. George Thomas expressed it succinctly: "Faith without reason is uncritical; reason without faith is uncreative."[14] Religious believers usually consider the moral beliefs of their religion fully consonant with moral reasoning.

One more value of reason for both believer and nonbeliever is that of being able to combine it with other ways of knowing. Reason can be joined with emotions, feelings, and intuitions. Gustafson sees discernment in moral judging as a process both rational and affective. The values of embracing reason are greater than this treatment captures, for rationality is basic to being human. In asking just why one should be rational, one is already acknowledging that one should be rational.

But, to move to the other side, reason does have its limitations. Previously, five limitations were noted:

1. Reason is only one way of making moral judgments; society's rules, facts about human nature, emotions, imag-

ination, feelings, intuitions, stories, and poetry are other ways.

2. Reason may actually have little to do with moral motivations, actions, and commitments; reason seldom moves people to moral action.

3. Reason is unable to solve disagreements between moral philosophers and theorists; pure and impartial reason do not seem to exist.

4. Reason can be used well; it can also be terribly misused. Humans can reason themselves into believing all kinds of ideas (the process we call rationalization). People who see themselves as rational can be very biased and prejudiced.

5. Reason does not stand alone, but is dependent on communities, traditions, and worldviews. All moral reasoning is culturally conditioned. MacIntyre's observations about different understandings of rationality seem valid.

Looking at reason from a larger perspective, a few additional limitations of reason become apparent:

Reason can lead to a moral skepticism and end up declaring that moral knowledge is impossible to achieve. Analytic philosophy contends that we have no objective (i.e., scientific) moral knowledge. And to say that we can never go from description to prescription, from an *is* to an *ought*, from a fact to a value, hinders the acquiring of moral knowledge. Bernard Williams persuasively argues that rational reflection by itself does not produce the moral confidence we need and desire.[15]

Expertise in moral reasoning does not automatically lead to moral living. Facts alone, rationally convincing as they may be, seldom if ever lead people to action. Concern for others is more important than moral reasoning in making people moral. Action is more important than reasoning. The Hindu law of karma says that we become good by doing good, not by talking about what is good. This observation also pertains to liberation theology, which operates not by searching for a theory of truth and then proceeding deductively, but through applying truths and values to human practice. Practice and action are more valuable than theory and reason, a view ordinary people often proclaim.

The Greeks, who are given much credit for their emphasis on reason, did not concentrate on reason to the exclusion of everything else. Edith Hamilton believes that the Greeks combined reason and spirit, the outer and the inner, reason and emotion.[16] The Greek virtue of moderation in all things is a worthy model, an example worth considering. When reason is put into perspective, the relationship between religion and morality can flourish.

Commonalities in Religious and Philosophical Ethics

After looking at the diversity within philosophical ethics at the end of chapter 3, seven points of agreement among philosophical ethicists were briefly noted. At this juncture, it seems appropriate to mention that the points on which philosophical ethicists agree are points that religious and philosophical ethics have in common. The beliefs and concerns that religious and philosophical ethics share are worth highlighting, and the relational approach to religion and morality helps us to lift up the common ground of religious and philosophical ethics.

What I find interesting is that religious and philosophical ethics have similar weaknesses as well as similar strengths. Among the most salient similar weaknesses are the conflicts one discovers within religious and philosophical ethics. In both, one finds a reluctance to deal with disagreements and an accompanying unwillingness to entertain different points of view. Both religious and philosophical ethics frequently fail to recognize how greatly each of them has been influenced by its respective cultural background and traditions.

Religious and philosophical ethics also share significant strengths. As mentioned, they have numerous common beliefs, beyond the seven points of agreement already noted. Their agreement on the importance of morality in human life is crucial and a fine starting point for dialogue. There is a definite dynamic in both that engenders a willingness to change and grow, which is admirable. Thus, despite the obvious differences between religious and philosophical ethics, in the long run the things they share are considerably more important. Because of this, a continuing relation between them should be encouraged.

Critical Openness

A relational approach is preferable because it fosters an attitude that is called "principled pluralism"[17] and "critical openness."[18] This attitude represents another middle way between two extremes often witnessed when different or opposite views confront each other. The first extreme is that of a dogmatic rejection or repudiation, a narrow exclusivism that absolutely refuses to have anything to do with a different viewpoint. The opposite extreme is that of an uncritical acceptance, a lazy-minded tolerance, a facile relativism, a sloppy inclusivism. Both of these popular extremes are undesirable. The first is usually found among religious, political, and moral fundamentalists and some conservatives. The second is found among some fuzzy-minded liberals and, according to the late Allan Bloom in *The Closing of the American Mind,* among most college and university students. The middle way of principled pluralism and critical openness contains characteristics that are constructive for religious and philosophical ethics, and for religious and secular persons.

A principled pluralism and critical openness enables persons to be open to truth and wisdom wherever it may be found. No individual understands or knows everything. It is altogether likely that our enemies and opponents understand things we have not yet grasped. Gandhi, for example, strongly believed that his opponents were not devoid of truth. A truly liberal person should be open to all truth—philosophical, aesthetic, scientific, and religious. Truth is often spoken of as one, the unity of truth. Valid as this may be, the emphasis here is simply on being receptive to truth, whatever its source.

Being open does not mean naively believing any idea that comes along, for a critical openness includes a commitment to the highest and best truth a person can accept and understand at a given time. In order to be critically open, a person must take a stand somewhere, must have a point of reference from which to be critical. Only those with some sort of identity, who to some extent know who they are and what they believe and value, are truly able to exercise critical openness. It is doubtful that a person lacking such an identity will be secure enough for genuine openness.

A critical openness necessitates a willingness to actively listen to the views and beliefs of those whose values and understandings of reality are different from our own. A critical openness also requires an acceptance of the possibility of understanding across barriers of time, place, and culture. Anthropologists are convinced that this kind of understanding is achievable.[19] A critical openness may also include a willingness to change our minds and hearts (often called *metanoia,* from the Greek) if the truth we discover is sufficiently compelling.

A principled pluralism and critical openness also makes it possible for opposing sides to provide insights and ideas that the other side needs and wants. Harold Best has observed that true pluralism is relational; it enhances the sharing of values and standards of excellence, and provides a nurturing intercourse in which communities learn from each other.[20] The old adage that says that it is better to argue with adversaries than to ignore them makes the same point.

A few examples may help: In being critically open, philosophers, humanists, and scientists often come to realize that there is wisdom in religious traditions, and that manifestations of truth, beauty, and goodness are discoverable in many places. On the other hand, religious ethicists may come to realize their need of the secular expertise that comes from social scientists and the philosophical vigor found in philosophical ethics.

The approach advocated here is especially valuable in enabling us to understand that borrowing from adversaries has been going on for a long time. In *The Origins of Christian Morality*, Wayne Meeks shows how similar the language of early Christianity was to that of the pagan philosophers and orators of the larger society. Meeks claims that it is difficult to say just when Christian ethics became distinctively Christian because of the "whirl of syncretism" in which it existed, and he concludes with the judgment that there has never been a purely Christian morality.[21]

A principled pluralism and critical openness is desirable because it is ethical—it is right and good to so operate. This approach is really an application of the Golden Rule, treating our opponents the way we would like them to treat us. It involves accepting others in ways we wish them to accept us. It is the most ethical way of dealing with relationships between religious and philosophical ethics. It may also be the most fruitful and pragmatic. William Sloane Coffin says it well: "We can build a community out of seekers for truth, not out of possessors of truth."[22]

Further examples of the acceptance or nonacceptance of principled pluralism can be mentioned. On the acceptance side, there is the statement quoted in chapter 4 of a supposed atheist, Mikhail Gorbachev, who said that the moral values of religion can help renew human societies. The Global Declaration of the Parliament of the World's Religions addressed itself to nonreligious people and all inhabitants of this planet, calling on all humans to work together on a global ethic. On the nonaccepting side, there is the late Christian theologian Dietrich Bonhoeffer, who claimed that Christian ethics and moral philosophy are utterly distinct, and that Christians should focus on the teachings and call of Jesus Christ. Perhaps if Bonhoeffer had lived into our time and witnessed the moral crises of our day, he would have become less insistent on this score. Still, we see that attractive as principled pluralism and critical openness appears to many, to others it seems dangerously close to relativism.

The Positive Role of Religion

The relational approach has another value—that of fostering an appreciation of the ongoing significance of religion in human life. Because the relational approach views religion and morality as complementary, it is more open to religion as a worthwhile human activity. The inseparable approach tends to tie morality so closely to religion that religion can be inhibited from expressing its many-dimensional nature. The separable approach, on the other hand, readily lends itself to views that make religion superfluous and that concentrate exclusively on morality. A relational approach preserves the positive role of religion.

To claim that religion exercises a constructive role in society is not to deny that religion as well as other worthwhile human activities (e.g., science, law, and politics) sometimes embody negative influences. All religions, or rather members of all religions, have engaged in conduct that most people now find morally unacceptable, such as slavery and racism. But even these negatives cannot completely erase the positive aspects of the religions in which humans have participated. As Jane Eyre so rightly points out: "To attack self-righteousness is not to assail religion."[23]

The positive role of religion was addressed in the sevenfold description of religion given in chapter 1. The parts of religion are human, prevalent, and positive. As human beings, we engage in believing and trusting in reality and the sacred, seek answers to life's deepest questions, encounter and experience ultimate reality, desire a relationship with the transcendent, value comprehensively and intensely, yearn for self-transformation, and look for supportive communities. I believe that these aspects of religion will continue to have meaning for human beings, thus enhancing the positive role of religion in a society in which negative reactions to religion seem to be growing.

Beyond the parts of religion previously mentioned, I wish to suggest four additional evidences of religion's positive role:

First, religion continues to have a positive moral influence in the lives of many people; it definitely influences behavior and actions. Because of the moral dimension found in religions, it is natural that the moral values that accompany religion affect to some extent the members of a religious tradition. The experiences, stories, teachings, and rituals that are dimensions of religion stir people to moral action. Religion addresses people at a deep level, that of motivation and will, the level that moves people to live out their moral ideals. This is precisely what makes religion a way of life and in the process blurs the line between religion and morality. It also points to what might be called a paradox, for even though religion transcends morality by being much more than morality, religion also undergirds morality. Religion supports proper conduct, anthropologist Clifford Geertz affirms, by picturing a world in which such conduct makes sense.[24] All this, sociobiologist Nicholas Ruse claims, shows that religion is useful even if it is an illusion.[25]

Some of the ways in which religion exercises a constructive moral influence on its members are apparent:

—Religion may provide, according to Niebuhr and Gustafson, a special moral sensitivity, a special awareness of the moral implications of different issues and events (e.g., the emphasis on compassion within religion makes people aware of acts that affect others in special ways).

—Religion offers its members communities in which they can learn and grow, as Rabbi Kushner emphasizes. A secular philosopher observes that religion is really morality's chief ally, for its members are encouraged to discuss important moral issues on a regular basis.[26]

—Religion motivates people to care for others, as philosophy does not. Religious communities call members to lives of love and concern, moving them to be generous and compassionate. In a recent study of charitable giving in the United States, Donald Shriver discovered that most charitable giving comes from religious groups, and that the lower- and middle-income members of these groups are more generous than upper-class people, whose religious affiliations are often very weak.[27]

Second, the positive role of religion can sometimes be found in nonreligious people. This sounds paradoxical, but it is a way of saying what sociologists of religion generally acknowledge—that religion exists in secularized form in modern societies. Some of the dimensions of religion (experiential, mythical, doctrinal, ethical, ritual, and social) are present, even if unobserved. A residue or deposit of religion remains when the forms of traditional religion have disappeared. Humanism, although critical of much religion, has called itself a religion, viewing itself as embodying the best of what religions provide. If religion is defined broadly—as Japanese philosopher Kitaro Nishida renders it, "thinking seriously"[28]— or as that which helps give meaning to the universe and life,[29] then religion will continue to exist in modern societies, in diverse and untraditional ways.

Beyond the above, it is suggested that agnostics and atheists can be influenced by religious morality in ways they are not aware of (e.g., through their conscience), and that atheists can be implicitly religious. After all, it is difficult to practice love and concern for others if one does not believe one should. Basil Mitchell has persuasively argued that Western culture has been greatly influenced by Christian views of the nature and predicament of humans. He also contends that morality, as traditionally conceived, because of Jewish and Christian influences is often not comfortable with secular worldviews and the humanisms of our day (scientific, romantic, and liberal). These humanisms do not offer adequate support for the intuitions of a traditional conscience. Mitchell believes that people with such a conscience may be more religious than they realize.[30]

Third, the continuing positive role of religion can be observed in religions that have learned to work together. Religious groups today are more aware than in times past that other religious communities exist. Richard Tarnas comments that religious sensibility is being revitalized in our day by its own plurality.[31] A poly-religious situation now exists in every large city; the number of diverse religious groups in these cities is almost impossible to calculate.

A striking example of this development, the *Declaration of a Global Ethic,* has been mentioned here a few times. This *Declaration* shows religions working together in discovering their commonalities, that common core of moral values that will benefit humanity. This coming together on moral values is a great step forward for humanity.

And this step forward has happened because many religious traditions have become more self-critical and less dogmatic. It seems to me that religious groups are not in any significant degree more dogmatic than some very ideological political groups. Many people of religious faith struggle with their doubts and unbelief, which enables them to be less doctrinaire and more flexible than some others.

Fourth, another evidence of the continuing positive role of religion is the role of religion in public and political life. This particular role is often looked on unfavorably by intellectuals in modern society, who prefer to confine religion's role to the private and individual sphere. Religious groups however, continue to play a legitimate and constructive role in public affairs. How is this true?

To begin, religious groups, along with other social groups, teach morality, and in the process prepare people for public life. The fact that public good depends on private virtues is acknowledged. The republican virtues of patience, temperance, prudence, and industry are the prior conditions of a democracy. Since these virtues are usually based on loyalty to a transcendent order—to something greater than ourselves—the assistance of religious groups in inculcating these virtues is apparent.

Historians generally agree that religion has been an important factor in history, particularly in American history. In order to understand American culture, the role of religion must be considered. Many of the earliest colonists came to this country expressly because of their religious beliefs. Many American events, such as the antislavery and civil rights movements, were loaded with religious beliefs and moral values that came from these beliefs. Several American Presidents, as previously noted, saw religion and morality as necessary for good government. Franklin Gamwell has a point when he claims that although the civil order cannot explicitly affirm one religious faith, it cannot be entirely neutral about religious faith either.[32]

In this context, it is relevant to mention the theory of a French sociologist, Emile Durkheim, who argued that religion functions as the creator and maintainer of social solidarity. Durkheim contended that all societies are built on some religious foundational myth, which acts with symbolic force in organizing the various phases of communal life.

The role of religion in society also bears on the question about the relationship of religion and politics, church and state. The prevailing view is that they should be completely separate, but in the *Encyclopedia of Religion,* Max L. Stackhouse cogently argues that religion influences politics as much as politics influences religion. Because politics requires power, as well as purpose and a vision that is accepted as authoritative, politics needs religion. In order to accept a political system as authoritative, people must see vision and purpose in it. Politics itself puts into place both nonpolitical and nonphilosophical values. Political authority seems incomplete without religion, which Stackhouse defines as a governing metaphysical-moral vision. As Max Weber saw, politics is ever subject to religious forces beyond its capacity to control. Political activity takes place in a socioreligious framework of authority that limits the range of possibilities. Therefore, politics must be seen in relation to religion, not as a simply autonomous human activity. As religion is a guarantee of legitimacy, religion is able to legitimate, inform, and renew society. Religion must be reckoned with, for the conflicts of our time cannot be understood without reference to religion (as, for example, the Iranian revolution and the conflict in northern Ireland). Stackhouse further shows the ways in which religion affects politics, as well as the political significance of a religious worldview in different religions. A total separation of religion and politics is probably impossible.[33]

If Stackhouse's arguments have any credibility, the American doctrine of separation of church and state needs interpretation. Separation may not be the best word—the word itself is not in the Constitution, but in a letter written by Thomas Jefferson. To be sure, because of the first amendment on religious freedom, it is doubtful that any American will strive for an arrangement whereby a church or a religion controls the state, or vice versa. In this sense, separation is desirable. But if separation denies the value of interaction and dialogue between religions and the civil order, then separation has become *separationism,* another unfortunate *ism.* The arguments of Kent Greenawalt and Stephen L. Carter, as mentioned, demonstrate religion's ongoing positive role in political life. If religion and morality should not be totally separated, religion and politics should not be completely separated either. Our common political life is laden with moral issues (for example, war, trade, health care, crime prevention, pollution). The moral dimension of religion places a heavy responsibility on religious groups to help people deal with the pressing moral problems of our time. Vaclav Havel is correct in saying, "All genuine politics has a moral origin."[34]

The Role of Faith

The relational approach recognizes the role of faith in both religion and morality. In this context, faith means accepting beliefs that cannot be proved but which we nevertheless have reasons for believing. Faith in this sense is responding to evidence or reasons. There are two ways in which an approach open to the role of faith is especially relevant.

First, faith is important to morality, as it is to religion. Faith is really basic to any system of morality, whether religiously or philosophically shaped. Codes of morality are accepted by people on faith—no other grounding or justification is considered necessary. Implicit convictions are present in moral behavior. Our reasons for being moral are not provided by moral reasoning, but by our underlying commitments. Our deepest values and beliefs are not scientifically provable. The rules of conduct that we accept presuppose belief. Explaining to anyone, even ourselves, why we should be moral often becomes frustrating, for rational justifications seldom suffice. Just why we should care about others, or why certain moral principles are "overriding" (a favorite word of philosophical ethicists), is difficult to explain without appealing to belief. To affirm, as moral philosophers have, that all human beings should have equal rights is not empirically verifiable. Perhaps this is why Frankena called for moral postulates.[35] Sociobiologists like Nicholas Ruse, who see morality as connected to genetics, admit that they have no ultimate reason for saying why people should act morally. Ruse acknowledges that morality becomes objective because people believe it is; it works because of human belief. Sociobiologists have argued that altruism is genetically caused, even though natural selection hardly seems adequate for explaining altruistic behavior toward nonkin.[36] As we have noted, even though Kant wanted morality to be autonomous and free from religious beliefs, he resorted to calling for an objective moral order and belief in God, freedom, and immortality. Furthermore, intuitional moral theory, which argues that a direct apprehension of moral truth is possible, suggests a role for faith. Hare acknowledges that persons who seek to be moral need to believe that the world is sympathetic to moral striving.[37] Also relevant is Haught's conclusion that persistent ethical enthusiasm requires belief.[38]

Second, faith is also important when we deal with reality and knowledge, metaphysics and epistemology. All worldviews, religious or secular, call for an ultimate commitment. It has often been noted that atheists exercise faith, for if it cannot be proved that God exists, as is generally recognized, neither can it be proved that God does not exist. Thus, to affirm God's existence or nonexistence involves faith, in the sense initially stated. Though it seems paradoxical, antifaith presupposes faith. Alvin Plantinga contends that it is more accurate to speak of a different faith than to speak of the absence of faith. People do believe, and need to believe, in realities whose existence they cannot prove. A former Russian Communist commented that he stopped believing in God and believed in a bright future under Marxism. When he could no longer believe in this bright future, he wondered what he could believe.

An extreme form of skepticism called nihilism seems to have continuing appeal for many humans. Nihilism rejects all meaning, beliefs, and values, and declares that nothing can be known or believed. However, nihilism is self-refuting: it cannot justify its own point of view, for if nothing can be believed, then the view that nothing can be believed cannot be believed either. All human judgments are grounded in prior assumptions that are not questioned (what Plantinga calls "basic beliefs"). As Mary Midgley puts it, there are many presuppositions we choose to believe before we start disbelieving.[39] Michael Polanyi is correct when he notes that there is no guarantee against error, for knowing involves a commitment.[40] And commitment requires faith.

Views of Reality

A further value of the relational approach is that it highlights the significance of views of reality, or worldviews, for morality. The inseparable approach does recognize the importance of worldviews, but sometimes limits itself to a particular worldview. The separable approach, on the other hand, downplays worldviews and fails to realize their importance. Analytic philosophy actually declares that views of reality, or metaphysical beliefs, are nonsense because they are neither rational (matters of logic) nor empirical (matters of fact), thus reducing moral philosophy to an analysis of moral language. Not many modern moral philosophers totally embrace analytic philosophy, but a reluctance to make metaphysical statements prevails within modern philosophy.

The significance of views of reality, worldviews and metaphysics, can be defended.

First, views of reality are rather universal; human beings have worldviews, a metaphysics. Metaphysics literally means "going beyond the physical," and points to the ground out of which physical existence emerges and has its being. Mary Midgley argues that we cannot get rid of metaphysics, because it is a necessary condition of extended thought. As a conceptual structure that underlies our world picture, metaphysics provides a general map of the world and universe and how they came to be.[41] Most humans are comfortable with a view of the universe as a place of order and purpose rather than as a place of chaos. Meaningful views about the world and human nature are desirable.

Second, views of reality are culturally conditioned, connected to traditions and communities. Human beings belong to languages, traditions, communities, and cultures. Moral selves are formed within communities and cultures. Further, cultures have moral traditions that include moral reasoning. Morality and science, as well as religion, are culturally shaped. Jürgen Habermas echoes this point by contending that what is real for us is that which can be experienced according to the interpretation of a symbolic system.[42] Symbolic systems are parts of the cultures and communities in which moral formation takes place. This means that some humans adopt worldviews that owe little to religion, and other humans adopt views that owe much to religion.

Third, since we live in a world of many worldviews, humans are exposed to various understandings of reality. Pluralism is one of the great facts of our time. The five worldviews articulated by Walter Wink continue to attract inhabitants of this planet. Human beings are drawn to different understandings of reality, sometimes to more than one worldview. Since a principled pluralism is desirable, we need not be completely controlled by our culture or by one particular worldview. Humans can criticize worldviews.

Views of reality are not necessarily mutually exclusive, but they can be somewhat incompatible. The materialistic and spiritualistic worldviews of Wink's scheme are not compatible. Basil Mitchell correctly observes that reflective people are aware of the need to choose between worldviews.[43] It may be impossible to seek a neutral stance between the theological and materialistic worldviews; a choice must be made.

Although contemporary philosophers, with increasing exceptions, consider metaphysics a shady area, it has become clear that metaphysical thinking is unavoidable. Those who reject one worldview do so because they accept a different understanding of reality. Tarnas seems on target in his view that those who view reality as fragmented rather than as integrated (e.g., deconstructionists) have their own justifying principles or metaphysics.[44] Views of reality and the criteria used in selecting them are matters of choice. And, as William James pointed out, since reality is very complex and thus greater than our ideas about it, humility in choosing is appropriate.

Fourth, our moral values and principles imply an understanding of reality. We can probably agree that morality can exist without religion, but it is highly unlikely that morality can exist without views of reality or worldviews. Religion cannot exist without a worldview or metaphysics.

Among voices in contemporary philosophy advocating the importance of metaphysics for morality, that of Iris Murdoch is clear and consistent. In a title that speaks for itself, *Metaphysics as a Guide to Morals*, she makes telling points on this subject. Murdoch affirms that moral energy is a function of how we see the world, and that when we reflect on morality we cannot avoid picturing the world. Consciousness and imagination have obvious moral dimensions. In a Platonic spirit, Murdoch embraces the good or goodness as a transcendental reality. She declares that the view that values do not exist, or cannot be known, is a clear metaphysical belief. Values actually provide the way we view the reality of the world.[45]

Many philosophers agree with Murdoch's view that morality presupposes views of reality. Holmes Rolston III says that ethics attaches itself to a worldview. Ian Barbour states that the value of individuals and respect for nature are values that depend on understandings of ultimate reality. Robert Wuthnow notes that implicit values guide most scientific research, and Charles Taylor says that ethics is connected to the meaning of nature and human existence. A renowned Indian philosopher, Sarvepalli Radhakrishnan, maintained that an ethical theory must be grounded in metaphysics, a philosophical concept of the relation between human conduct and ultimate reality. As we think ultimate reality to be, so we behave.[46]

The fact that the three great thinkers of Western moral philosophy—Aristotle, Kant, and Mill—have definite metaphysical beliefs has been described. All theories—moral, political, aesthetic, literary, and philosophical—have presuppositions that are not philosophically and religiously neutral. In contemporary America, many journalists, politicians, academics, and clergy complain loudly about the decline of moral values and the lack of a moral compass among people today. It may well be that this phenomenon is connected to the changing views of reality and the secularization of American life, as noted by some sociologists. The search for a new metaphysics of quality (as seen in Pirsig) that can provide meaning and morality without employing traditional religion also shows the importance of metaphysics and worldviews for morality. The fascination with New Age religion is another indication of people looking for satisfactory views of reality. And the growing protest against environmental degradation may have moral and metaphysical implications—moral in the sense that we ought to do better (clean up our act), and metaphysical in the sense that this is not what the universe was intended to be. James Hunter has observed that for some humanists a high view of nature or the social order is functionally equivalent to an objective and transcendent order.[47]

Natural Law Theory as a Bridge

A relational approach has a further merit, that of making possible the utilization of natural law theory as a bridge between religious and philosophical ethics. In chapter 3, a brief description of natural law ended with the suggestion that this theory could serve as a mediator between religious and philosophical ethics. Natural law as a constructive alternative can be defended.

The theory of natural law has the advantage of being open to both religious and philosophical perspectives: it emphasizes reason (philosophical) and allows for revelation and faith (religious). Openness need not imply total agreement, for natural law theory is capable of being critical of both religious and philosophical ethics. Natural law theory does not agree with the forms of divine command theory, which tend to condemn the use of reason. Nor does it accept the view of analytic philosophy that moral statements indicate nothing more than the emotions of the moral speaker (the emotive theory). In this respect, natural law ethics may be able to develop a wholesome relation between religious and philosophical ethics.

As natural law theory evolved during the Middle Ages, following the significant contribution of Thomas Aquinas, it may have prepared the way for philosophical ethics to stand on its own. Aquinas believed that God prohibited certain things, such as murder and theft, because they are wrong in themselves, not simply because God declared them forbidden. In opposition to William of Ockham, Aquinas argued that things are right and wrong in themselves, thus answering Socrates's question in *Euthyphro* the way Socrates might have answered it. In so doing, Aquinas paved the way for philosophical ethics to declare its independence from religion, the move subsequently forwarded by Kant and Mill.

A salient fact in this context is the recognition that Christian ethics has often been sympathetic to natural law theory. This is especially true among Catholic moral philosophers and theologians who respect Aquinas. But Protestant moral philosophers, such as Paul Ramsey, H. Richard Niebuhr, James M. Gustafson, and Paul Tillich, have also been receptive to natural law thinking. Natural law theory fits well with H. Richard Niebuhr's relational model of Christian ethics, in which humans are regarded as responders and dialoguers rather than as makers (teleological theory) or citizens (deontological theory).

It is only fair to add that many Protestant ethicists have been critical of natural law ethics. Their opposition is largely based on the view that natural law theory relies on human reason, one of the human faculties susceptible to corruption and misuse. Nevertheless, natural law theory continues to be employed by both religious and philosophical ethicists.

Natural law theory has an impressive history. Its roots are in Greek and Roman philosophy—Plato, Aristotle, the Stoics, and Cicero were among its primary proponents. Aquinas's contributions have been noted. John Locke used natural law theory also, and subsequently influenced Thomas Jefferson in this direction. Natural law theory has been an important aspect of Western religious and philosophical history. The theory has never lacked critics, but since the proponents of this theory can themselves be critical of the theory, natural law theory continues to exist and evolve.

Natural law theory has merit in its emphasis on the rationality that humans share. It regards humans as uniquely capable of reasoning and having a rational understanding of moral laws and rules. According to this theory, there are moral principles that all "mature" beings can understand which are written on the heart.[48] Kohlberg's sixth and penultimate stage of moral development is that "of any rational individual recognizing the nature of morality or the basic moral premise of respect for other persons as ends, not means."[49] Natural law elements are readily detectable in this statement. Imperfect as reason may be, its role in morality endures and natural law theory reinforces this approach.

Natural law theory also emphasizes a common human nature. Some will deny that a human nature exists. We cannot deal with this issue here, but simply call attention to the contention of natural law theory that there is a human nature, however difficult it may be to say precisely what that means. Natural law theorists believe that ideas of right and wrong and good and evil are located within human nature. Standards of morality are thus found within human nature (often called autonomy) and not in something found outside of human nature (heteronomy). Reason, feeling, and will are important parts of human nature, which has both an outer and an inner side. The outer side, which can be scientifically studied and interpreted, may provide what Adler calls the facts of human nature, as well as a partial understanding of human existence, which is where ethical reflection begins, according to Gustafson.[50]

The inner side of human nature is less observable. Perhaps this is why behavioral psychologists ignore it and concentrate on behavior. But the inner side of human nature is crucial for morality and ethics. The inner side is known as people become aware of their inner states, the data of their own consciousness, thoughts, and feelings. Buddhists have stressed the importance of such an awareness. W. W. Bartley III also contends that the inner side of humans is most important for morality. In this connection, he takes vehement exception to what he calls a British view, that religion concerns one's attitudes toward the ultimate and one's inner states, while morality is directed toward the outside world and the intermediate. He claims that this differentiation is entirely too sharp, because morality also requires self-knowledge and awareness of inner states. Morality is not restricted to social behavior—it also relates to inner beliefs. Bartley rightly contends that only those people aware of their inner states and the evil they are capable of committing are actually capable of doing great good.[51] Bartley's view constitutes another cogent argument for religion and morality as relational.

The emphasis of natural law theory on human nature is helpful because it enables us to better understand that as humans we are moral beings, moral selves, and moral agents. But we are moral beings before we are moral agents and actors—being precedes doing. As reflective beings, in our consciousness we consider the kind of people we want to be, what we ought to do, what is right and good. Morality will always be an integral part of being human, a central aspect of human nature. The fact that natural law theory focuses on human nature gives it merit, even if the theory is partially flawed.

Another value of natural law theory as a mediator between religious and philosophical ethics is its willingness to use science. The relationship of science and ethics is debatable. Some views about possible relationships were discussed in chapter 3. Since the discussion concluded by affirming a possible relationship, it seems fitting to lift up some ways in which natural law theory makes effective use of science.

It does so, first, by looking to science for help in describing human nature, getting the facts of human nature. The two sciences that do this well are biology and psychology. The emergence of sociobiology, with its explanations of morality and altruism as products of genetic endowment, has been somewhat enlightening. Many moral philosophers have used Lawrence Kohlberg's work on the psychology and philosophy of moral development. That natural law theory is open to science is to its credit.

A second way in which natural law theory makes constructive use of science is in seeking to go beyond the fact/value, is/ought dichotomy. Many moral philosophers have been eager to find a way of overcoming the "naturalistic fallacy." While admitting the real difficulty of going from an *is* to an *ought*, both religious and philosophical ethicists feel that there are times when it is legitimate to do so. Not many will agree with Robert Veatch, who declares that the very *is* of human nature has an *ought* built into it, and that we discover what we ought to do by understanding the facts about human nature.[52] Callahan has observed that many scientists today recognize that there are probably no facts without values, for no matter how objective they strive to be, scientists cannot avoid making value judgments. If science need not be value-free, than values need not be science-free either.[53]

The developing field of applied ethics called environmental or ecological ethics provides an example. As experts from different sciences made public their findings about pollution of air, soil, and water and environmental degradation in general, moral philosophers began to realize the urgency of doing something about this crisis. Here is an obvious case of facts leading to values, description going on to prescription. This inclination of people to speak about facts *or* values is another demonstration of the human propensity to take black or white, either/or approaches when prudence requires a both/and approach. If natural law theory helps us to do the latter, it is worthy of our consideration.

Natural law theory has value in yet another regard: it can engender a respect for nature. This may seem questionable, for it is difficult to agree with Thomas Jefferson's claim that there is a moral order in the structure of nature itself. Since nature often appears "red in tooth and claw" (life feeds on life), his claim seems hard to believe. Nature does, however, show us that what we sow is what we reap. The fact that actions have consequences has a moral ring to it. We seem to be learning that when we abuse nature we will have to endure the consequences.

Daunting though it may be to find moral patterns in nature itself, it is interesting that moral philosophers embracing a naturalistic, humanistic ethic, who look to human nature and possibly nature itself as the source of moral value, also use the concept of creation with regard to nature. Secular moral philosophers sometimes talk about creation and the idea of stewardship—the idea that the earth does not belong to us, but has been given to us to manage and care for wisely. Stewardship and creation were originally religious beliefs. If in the process of secularizing religious beliefs moral theories enhance a respect for nature, it may not be necessary to dwell on the religious background of these concepts.

As might be expected, some religious ethicists want to go farther. Gustafson, for example, believes that nature tells us about God, and that since science helps us learn about nature, we should learn from science how nature works and thrives.[54] His proposal appeals to both religious and philosophical ethicists.

One more advantage of natural law theory is its general employability. This theory continues to appeal to different people in different times and places. It has been used, for example, by our founding fathers. When Thomas Jefferson wrote in the Declaration of Independence that "we hold these truths to be self-evident," he was making use of natural law. The Nuremberg trials also utilized natural law, by pointing to higher laws than those found within the positive laws of the countries involved. Martin Luther King Jr. also used natural law theory in distinguishing between just and unjust laws, those which should be obeyed versus those which should not be obeyed.

The above arguments are designed to show why natural law theory continues to attract people who seek a middle way, who want to combine the best of religious and philosophical ethics. The emphasis in natural law on prudence and discernment is acceptable to the religious as well as the nonreligious. Natural law is also employed by theologians pursuing what is called liberation theology, a theological movement that calls for action and the liberation of people from political, economic, educational, and other systems that prevent them from flourishing. The claim that natural law theory is open to an ethics of rules and principles as well as virtue ethics has also been made.[55] Most importantly, perhaps, is the claim that natural law theory is serviceable in the movement for a common morality.

If Mortimer J. Adler is correct in his view that the precepts of natural law are the same for all human beings, and that all human beings should have what is truly good for them (what they truly need), then natural law theory will appeal to those interested in a common morality.

Art and Morality

Another commendable feature of the relational approach, as opposed to the inseparable and separable approaches, is the way it helps us to realize that the activities we humans tend to separate should really be related. I have pleaded for a relationship between religion and politics as part and parcel of a relation between religion and morality. A relationship between art and morality is an additional benefit of the relational approach.

The activities we call art include many things—music, painting, sculpture, dance, literature, architecture, and more—that humans create for their enrichment, enjoyment, and contemplation. To say that art is a valuable part of being human seems an understatement.

However, the fact of distrust between art and religion is also obvious. The distrust is often mutual. Nevertheless, because artistic and religious experiences have similarities, it can be argued that art can enhance both religion and morality in very positive ways.

This assertion is relevant to a discussion of art and morality. While acknowledging that works of art can convey immoral influences, the positive role of art in fostering morality can be highlighted. Aesthetics, the philosophy of art, has several theories that focus on this possibility: art as insight into reality; art as an expression and communication of truth about self, the world, and reality; and art as an expression of high moral values, which Leo Tolstoy advocated.

The special significance of literature as an art that can enhance morality is what I wish to emphasize. The American novelist Walker Percy says that great writing is moral—it deals with pathology and health. According to Percy, all outrage is moral.[56] The idea that literature can have a moral purpose is only one literary theory among others, but it seems to me that both religious and philosophical ethicists should listen to literary as well as other artists. Just as with religion and morality, art and morality should not be totally inseparable or separable, but relational. An imaginative, creative morality, along with a morally sensitive art, represent ideals worth seeking.

A Common Morality

Lastly, a relational approach is definitely more conducive to the emergence of a common morality. In making religion and morality inseparable, the value of secular insights is slighted or denied. In totally separating religion and morality, religious and philosophical ethicists fail to communicate.

The relational approach is better, for it encourages equal input from religious and philosophical ethics toward the development of a common morality.

In the first place, this means that philosophical ethics should be open to religious ethics, the moral beliefs that spring from religion. As mentioned, being open does not mean facile agreement or lazy tolerance, but a critical appropriation of what is valuable, whatever its source. On the part of those who are receiving input from religious ethics, a spirit of openness signifies a willingness to encourage the kind of religious freedom that enables religions to exercise their public role, and not to confine religion and religious ethics to a private and individual role. This willingness will make it possible for religion to contribute to a public philosophy, core values, a common morality, or to what has been called the "public square." Os Guiness suggests three ways for talking about the public square: a *naked* public square (one in which all religions are excluded), a *sacred* public square (one in which one religion is established or semiestablished), and a *civil* public square (one in which members of all faiths are free to engage one another). All religions can work together for a civil public square, in which the public role of religion is accepted. Michael Harrington even proposed a united front of believers and atheists in the defense of good moral values.[57]

Religions that contribute to the public square have serious responsibilities. In their public role, Martin Marty proposes that religions not invoke privilege, but look for stories they can share with nonreligious citizens. Religions can defend their particular moral teachings; they should also support a more general morality. In order to speak to the public square, religious traditions must be convinced of the need for a moral consensus, a common morality, a global ethic. They must speak truthfully and forthrightly, bearing witness to their beliefs and convictions. They must also seek ways of communicating with people who speak other moral languages. Religions must try to get their act together and work out some of their differences. They must also be aware of religious pluralism and realize that no one religious group can dominate. Any unity achieved in their efforts will be a unity with diversity. Religions must also support the voices of minorities within their communities, such as women, third world citizens, ethnic minorities, and so forth. Above all, religions must seek points of agreement with other religions, focusing on what they have in common. The Parliament of the World's Religions provides a fine example of how religions can discover their commonalities and contribute to a global ethic.

Equal input also means that religious ethicists must be open to philosophical ethicists, to the moral insights coming from secular ethics. As noted, this places responsibilities on both the giver and the receiver. As receivers, the religious traditions must be willing to do a number of things:

—Be open to the truth, whatever its source;

—Be sympathetic to the moral beliefs of those who do not share their religious beliefs;

—Realize that nonreligious people are fellow human beings. Even if they do not agree with these people, they can work with them for the improvement of our common life, the long-range goal of a common morality;

—Try to understand that a public philosophy cannot be expressed in religious language, and be willing to accept a moral language that can satisfy both religious and secular people;

—Deliberately attempt to express religious ethics in secular ways. Religious traditions must explore those moral values they have in common with nonreligious people, remembering that religious people can accept a general morality as well as their particular morality. American religious groups must recognize that for many Americans the so-called Judeo-Christian legacy does not really exist;

—Make serious efforts toward rational discussions with people whose views may be diametrically different;

—Practice civility;

—Understand that many people, both religious and secular, are deeply concerned about survival;

—Try to appreciate a view found in biblical faith—that God sometimes speaks and works through unbelievers, those whom Robert McAfee Brown calls "Assyrians in modern dress."

Naturally, the responsibilities given to religious ethicists above also apply to philosophical ethicists. A comparable humility and an eagerness to communicate and to seek those commonalities that can result in the common good are imperative.

Concluding Comments

In this chapter we have considered an array of arguments to support a relational approach. These arguments are not final or conclusive, but collectively I believe they are plausible and persuasive. I am personally persuaded that making religion and morality relational is the most constructive approach now available, and that if we adopt it, the results should be beneficial for the inhabitants of this planet, human and nonhuman.

What will happen if this relational approach is adopted? Some will quickly say: Nothing will happen! Because of unwillingness and sheer obstinacy on both sides, it will not even be attempted! Those who answer thus are convinced that neither religious nor philosophical ethicists will take the trouble to work for agreement and common ground. They will call their response realistic. It can also be called pessimistic, even cynical. The problem with both pessimism and optimism, as one of my teachers taught me, is that both decide the outcome in advance.

The attitude of hope is better, for it is realistic enough to fully realize the immense problems we face, yet confident that with serious and sincere efforts by people of goodwill things can change and positive progress can be made. I am personally hopeful that by adopting a relational approach, viewing religion and morality as neither inseparable nor separable, the possibilities of a common morality will increase. Only time will tell if this kind of hopefulness is warranted. In the meantime, we have everything to gain by proceeding with the view that religion and morality, or religious and philosophical ethics, are truly relational.

The concluding chapter, which deals with environmental ethics, constitutes one attempt to demonstrate the possibility and potential of a relational approach.

Chapter 7

Preserving Species

In previous chapters I developed two conclusions: religion and morality are best regarded as relational, rather than as inseparable or separable, and religious and philosophical ethics can converse and cooperate with each other. In this chapter I wish to put these conclusions to work on a specific moral issue, in order to test their fruitfulness. The chosen issue comes from an applied ethics field, that of environmental ethics, and has to do with the preservation of species (often called biodiversity).

In pursuit of this purpose a threefold approach is taken: First, the problem and situation that give rise to the particular moral issue are described. Second, the way philosophical and religious ethics address the particular issue is discussed. Third, ways in which religious and philosophical ethics can learn from and cooperate with each other in dealing with the stated issue are noted. If it is likely that religious and philosophical ethics can converse and cooperate on the specific moral issue, my conclusions are confirmed.

Environmental Ethics

Before pursuing the selected issue within environmental ethics, a brief description of environmental ethics is in order. Environmental ethics is one of the youngest fields of applied ethics—the branch of ethics that seeks to apply normative ethical theories to special concerns. Applied ethics relates theory to practice. The major concern of environmental ethics is how we should treat the environment, the natural, nonhuman world. Environmental ethics is based on the premise that an environmental crisis has surfaced in our time. Among the indicators of this crisis are pollution of air, water, and soil; depletion of the ozone layer; population growth that strains the carrying capacity of our planet; the difficulty of handling our refuse; the challenge to maintain adequate recreational space; the loss of nonrenewable resources (such as topsoil, oceanic life, and the extinction of many species); global warming, and so forth. Environmental ethics attempts to apply moral ideas to these problems.

Environmental ethics is a growing field. A reputable journal on environmental ethics has circulated since 1979, and new books in this field appear monthly. An International Society of Environmental Ethics publishes a widely distributed newsletter about developments in this field.

A significant aspect of environmental ethics lies in its heavy dependence on sciences, including chemistry, biology, ecology, geology, climatology, and academic disciplines such as economics. Scientists in these disciplines have made us aware of the crisis situation that environmental ethics and applied sciences are constructively engaging. Environmental ethicists seek to maintain close relations with natural and social scientists.

The Problem of Species Loss

The problem behind this moral issue is the increasingly alarming rate at which many animal and plant species are becoming extinct, totally lost. Natural scientists are convinced that variety and diversity within biological life, or biodiversity, are desirable. This is but one problem among many that environmental ethics addresses. This particular problem, however, is related to other environmental concerns, such as animal protection; loss of forests and farmland, wetlands and wilderness (habitat destruction); human population growth; and the pollution of air, soil, and water.

The annual reports called *State of the World* published by the Worldwatch Institute have focused on this issue. An article titled "Avoiding a Mass Extinction Crisis" noted that extinction crises have occurred previously, but the present crisis, set in motion by human activity and expanding population growth, is much swifter. Even in national parks, where animal life is safeguarded, species are being threatened. Another article, "Conserving Biological Diversity," claims that diversity is "collapsing at mind-boggling rates." Every species, including the human, is very dependent on others for its well-being. Two thirds of the world's plants are found in the tropics, where rain forests are rapidly being destroyed. Some of the destroyed plants may have had considerable medicinal value. The cost of species loss is greater than those concerned are able to calculate.[1]

In June 1996, the Food and Agricultural Organization of the United Nations held an International Technical Conference in Germany on Plant Genetic Resources. This conference called attention to several important facts: scientists do not know exactly how many species of plants and animals currently exist on earth, but do know the number is declining. Approximately 250,000 plant species have been identified, out of an estimated total of three hundred to five hundred thousand. Every day, according to environmental scientists, fifty plant and animal species disappear. In the past century and a half, the number of cultivated species has declined by about 75 percent. Genetic traits, such as resistance to disease, are being lost. Researchers believe that this fact could jeopardize humanity's ability to feed itself. At present, some 800 million people worldwide are under-nourished. World food production will have to increase by 75 percent of current levels over the next thirty years to keep pace with expected population growth.[2]

The problem of species loss has received political attention in recent years, nationally and internationally. In 1973, the United States Congress passed the Endangered Species Act, leading to some successes. The Rio Conference of the United Nations on Environment and Development in 1992 dealt with this by agreeing to an International Convention on Biological Diversity, which spoke of the "intrinsic value of biological diversity and of the ecological, genetic, social, economic, scientific, cultural, recreational and aesthetic values of biological diversity and its components." This convention also affirmed that biological diversity is a common concern for humankind that all nations should acknowledge and support.

Edward O. Wilson, the renowned entomologist of Harvard University, has been a leading proponent for biodiversity. He believes that the loss of biological diversity is the greatest scientific problem humanity faces today. This diversity, which took three billion years to develop, is seen by Wilson as our greatest asset. Wealth is material, cultural, and biological, and the latter is the most significant. Wilson declares that every scrap of biological diversity should be judged as valuable until we learn its use and come to a better understanding of what it means for humanity. This implies that no species should be allowed to become extinct. Interestingly, Wilson ends by going beyond science into morality, by calling for "an enduring ethic" that will attempt to preserve the health of all species.[3]

Philosophical Ethics and Biodiversity

The philosophical ethicists doing environmental ethics have two starting points: the first is an appreciation of science in general and natural sciences in particular. Science in general provides a basic narrative of how matter, life, and mind evolved in the universe. Thomas Berry and Brian Swimme call this "the universe story."[4] The story of science demonstrates that plant and animal life preceded human life—"they were here first." This aspect of the story of science has a bearing on the issue of biodiversity.

The natural sciences make a particular contribution to environmental ethics, especially the science of ecology, which investigates the interrelationships of organisms and their environment. Ian Barbour highlights four

prevailing concepts of ecology: (1) the ecosystem concept—the interconnected web of life; (2) the finite carrying capacity of the environment; (3)
ecological stability—reaching a dynamic balance is desirable; (4) long-
term spans of species deserve careful study.[5]

The second starting point of environmental ethics is an emerging consensus among environmental ethicists about the imperative to move beyond anthropocentrism—the tendency to center all values and actions in
what humans want and need. The attitude that nonhuman life (animals
and plants) exists for the economic and aesthetic use of humans has dom-
inated Western thinking. Nonhuman life exists for humans to exploit and
enjoy; it has no other purpose for existing. Anthropocentrism grants no
rights, good, or value to nonhuman life beyond that which humans allow.
Not all environmental ethicists agree with the proposal that plants and animals have rights and intrinsic value. They do seem to agree that humans
should cease making human wants and needs totally determinative in all
situations.

In considering the views of philosophical environmental ethicists, I pro-
pose looking at two of the major theories within philosophical ethics discussed in chapter 3: good-ends and duty/obligation theories, considering
first good-end theories as found in utilitarianism.

Beginning with utilitarianism seems appropriate in that the originators
of this theory, Bentham and Mill, had unusual ideas about duties to animals. They argued that humans have duties to animals because they are
sentient creatures; they have senses and feelings, and can experience pain
and suffering. The earliest utilitarians were willing to include animals in
their grand purpose of eliminating pain and fostering pleasure and happiness for as many creatures as possible. Whether Bentham and Mill
would have included insects and plants in their program is questionable.

At any rate, most modern utilitarians have moved toward a greater inclusivism. A worthy example is Peter Singer, an Australian philosopher
well known for his championing of animal liberation. Along with Tom Re-
gan, an ethicist who also works in a utilitarian framework, Singer has en-
thusiastically proclaimed animal rights. In his book *The Expanding Circle:
Ethics and Sociobiology* he asserts that "the sphere of altruism has broad-
ened from the family and tribe to the nation, race, and now to all human
beings. The process should now be expanded, as we have seen, to include
all beings with interests, of whatever species. But we cannot simply pro-
pose this as the ultimate ethical standard and then expect everyone to act
accordingly. We must begin to design our culture so that it encourages
broader concerns without frustrating important and relatively permanent
human desires."[6] In a similar vein, Singer's "strong utilitarianism" principle has often been noted: "If it is in our power to prevent something bad

from happening, without thereby sacrificing anything of comparable moral importance, we ought, morally, to do it."[7] Utilitarian ethicists will differ over Singer's proposals, but modern utilitarians seem to support the need to preserve as many species as possible.

Looking now at deontological, duty/obligation theories, we find little about biodiversity. Perhaps this is because the primary figure here is Immanuel Kant, who saw only duties pertaining to fellow humans. Nevertheless, I have wondered if we could extend Kant's theory about treating others as ends, not as means, and apply it to human treatment of the natural, nonhuman world. It is interesting that the popular Harvard biologist Stephen J. Gould has actually applied the Golden Rule to the natural world by saying that we should treat nature as we wish it to treat us.[8]

More substantially, Holmes Rolston III, a respected environmental ethicist, has written about duty to endangered species. His deliberate use of the word duty suggests a deontological approach. He calls it a prima facie duty, meaning that it can be overridden if necessary when dealing with things like pests and disease. However, the duty remains. A species, according to Rolston, is an inherent, ongoing form of life, expressed in organisms, encoded in gene flow, and shaped by the environment. Species have a history; their extinction shuts down the generative process, stops the historical gene flow along with crucial biological information. A lost individual is reproducible, a lost species is not. Consumption of individual animals and plants can be justified, consumption of a species cannot. If we should not kill the individuals of a species, Rolston says that killing of species is "superkilling." But what is advantageous to an individual may be advantageous to a species: attacking wolves may actually strengthen the remaining elks. Since species exist in ecosystems, we cannot protect systems without protecting ecosystems. To protect the spotted owl we had to also keep old-growth forests, which are valuable in themselves. As "moral overseers," Rolston contends that humans should value this host of species as something with a claim to care in their own right. They have value as objects of wonder and delight, not just for the experience of wonder they may give to humans. Rolston's case for duty to endangered species and biodiversity is persuasive.[9]

The moral issue of preserving species is not so easily settled, however, for the reason that a fairly strong division exists among environmental ethicists. They generally agree on the need to move beyond anthropomorphism. This agreement has led to a movement or school of thought called biocentrism or deep ecology. Deep ecologists, influenced largely by Aldo Leopold, argue that anything that preserves the biotic community is moral, anything that destroys the biotic community is immoral. Because the emphasis is on protecting life, this way of thinking is called biocentrism. All forms of life should be preserved and maintained. Deep ecology thus definitely favors biodiversity.

However, some environmental ethicists have problems with biocentrism. They argue that biocentrism puts all forms of life on the same level, and thus provides no help when decisions have to be made involving conflicts of life with life. These conflicts exist not only between humans and animals. They exist between animals themselves, and between animals and plants (e.g., conflict when a species of goats destroys a plant species in a certain locale). This situation has led some environmental ethicists to embrace Whitehead's philosophy of organism as a middle way between anthropocentrism and biocentrism. Whitehead's organic view of reality views reality as a network of interacting entities. Everything that exists is part of a larger whole, yet every individual entity is of value in and of itself. According to Whitehead, every creature is of value to itself, to others, and to God. Thus, all living things are valuable, but not equally so.

Kenneth Cauthen, in his study of Whitehead in relation to ethics, expressed it succinctly: "There is a hierarchy of intrinsic value. The greater the range, depth, intensity, complexity, and potential for enjoyment, the greater the inherent worth of the subject. A being has rights commensurate with potential for enjoyment. Hence, a person has more value than an animal, and an animal more than a plant. But all living beings have some degree of intrinsic value and a corresponding set of rights and claims for self-realization. Hence, not even a mosquito should be killed or a weed pulled up without justification. All morality begins with respect for life and its possibilities for enjoyment. In the very nature of things, life is in tragic conflict with itself. Organisms feed on other organisms, yet all life has intrinsic value, so that when life robs other life it can only be justified, if at all, when the lower serves the higher."[10]

The division between environmental ethicists illustrates the importance of metaphysics for ethics (as previously argued). What seems clear is that whether they proceed from a biocentric or organismic basis, philosophical environmental ethicists do agree on the need for biodiversity.

Religious Ethics
and Biodiversity

What one thinks about the need to preserve species largely depends on how one views the natural world and one's relation to it, which in turn significantly depends on a person's worldview (beliefs about the nature of reality). Worldviews are often connected to religious beliefs.

With these assertions in mind, we now consider some beliefs of the world's religions that have a bearing on biodiversity. We will consider three Western religions: Judaism, Christianity, and Islam; three Eastern religions: Hinduism, Buddhism, and Taoism; and Native American religions.

Judaism

The scriptures of the Jewish religion contain four major beliefs relevant to preserving species.

First, God created everything, all forms and species. Both creation stories of Genesis affirm the fundamental Jewish belief that God brought all that exists into being. The Talmud, a collection of rabbinic interpretations of Jewish scripture, says: "Of all that the Holy One created in his world, He did not create a single thing that is useless."[11]

Second, the writer of Genesis 1 has God declaring all creation good; all species are good as created. In philosophical language, all species are intrinsically valuable. They have value in themselves, not simply because humans value them. The famous Jewish physician and philosopher Maimonides commented that creation does not exist for our sake.[12] The Noah story of Genesis 6—9 suggests that God was eager to have two "of every kind" of animal and plant preserved in the ark. The things that God created and called good should be protected.

Third, Jewish scripture affirms that creation, the natural world, really belongs to God, not to humans or any other species. The psalmist declared that "The earth is the Lord's and all that is in it, the world, and those who live in it" (Ps. 24:1). As previously noted, all Western religions are theocentric (God-centered), not anthropocentric or biocentric. In the psalms, all things praise God (Ps. 104 and 148). Every creature has its own hymn of praise wherewith to extol the Creator.[13] In contrast to the desacralized world of moderns, the ancient Israelites saw God in the natural world. They did not *know* as much as we do about it, but actually lived closer to its rhythms. They joyfully celebrated nature, as in the Sukkoth festival. The Jewish Bible contains the story of a people who lived intimately with the land around them.[14] Their God was creator, sustainer, and redeemer, a truth that some biblical scholars have slighted.

Fourth, Jewish faith believes that humans were given the responsibility of caring for creation. The first creation story expresses this with the controversial word "dominion" (Gen. 1:28), the second story with the charge to "till" and "keep" the garden in which they lived (Gen. 2:15). The Hebrew word translated as dominion contains strong connotations of justice and caring. The point of these stories, however, is that although creation belongs to God, humans should lovingly tend it. Animals should be treated humanely, and plants (especially trees) should not be destroyed (Deut. 20:19). The idea that humans are given responsible management, often called stewardship, must be balanced with recognition of God's ultimate ownership. The idea of caring management should prevail, for Jews and others realized that if other species are to be protected and preserved, this will happen only when we accept responsibility to care for creation.

Christianity

As an offspring of Judaism, Christianity concurs with the four Jewish beliefs stated above. Christians faithful to their Jewish heritage will support species preservation. However, Christianity and Judaism have been criticized as antiecological. In an article published in 1967, a University of California historian, Lynn White, contended that Christianity is largely responsible for the environmental crisis of our day. White's argument is complex, but basically he maintained that Christianity promoted a science and technology that allowed humans to exploit the natural world in an ecologically disastrous manner.[15] Was White correct?

The present consensus is that White was partly right and partly wrong. It is true that Christianity has contributed to the desacralization of nature, and that Christians have emphasized the "dominion" as opposed to the "till and keep" role. Also, because of a lingering otherworldly attitude, Christians have often degraded nature and matter. Christian theologians like Origen, Aquinas, Luther, and Calvin have fostered anthropocentrism.

On the other hand, Christian theologians like Irenaeus, Augustine, and St. Francis have promoted a caring approach. Christians have often called for restrictions and restraints on dominion. Christians have also celebrated the beauty and bounty of the earth. Not all Christians have embraced animals and plants as intensely as St. Francis, but many Christians have sincerely appreciated and enjoyed nature as God's handiwork. The record is mixed, for Christian practices have often failed to match Christian ideals. Religious traditions, or religious people, will always need to be challenged to live up to their ideals.

When we study religions to learn of their ideals, it is helpful to consider their scriptures or origins, their historical development, and their present manifestations. The scriptures of Christianity focus on Jesus as the Christ/Messiah. Jesus actually said nothing directly about how his followers should treat the natural world. In his stories he often referred to humans who work with the world of nature—planting, harvesting, fishing, and tending flocks. His knowledge and appreciation of the natural world is striking: he spoke of the sun's benefiting all beings (Matt. 5:45), of how God cares for birds and plants (Matt. 6:25–30), and how seeds planted in the earth grow (Mark 4:26–32). Although Jesus did not speak to the issue we are considering, his caring-for-creation lifestyle provides an excellent model.

Almost half of the Christian writings in the Bible consist of Paul's writings. Paul did not deal with biodiversity, for he probably expected the present order to end soon. His otherworldliness precluded active interest in these concerns. However, in his letter to the Romans, Paul made comments that have a possible bearing on our discussion: In chapter 1:20 he stated that God can be "understood and seen through the things he has made." And in 8:21 he wrote that "creation itself will be set free from its bondage to decay and will obtain the freedom of the glory of the children of God." Paul apparently looked forward to the restoration of creation's original splendor and fullness. Anticipating such a restoration can influence Christians to care more about biodiversity here and now.

In Christianity's historical development, Christian theologians like Irenaeus and Augustine have highlighted the natural world, and Christians like St. Francis have shown an intense love for all creation. Christianity also had a Meister Eckhart, who wrote: "Apprehend God in all things, for God is in all things. Every single creature is full of God and is a book about God."[16] Eckhart represents a view called panentheism—God is in everything. This view has at times been popular in Christian thinking, and has achieved a renaissance in our day through Matthew Fox's "creation spirituality."

Present manifestations of Christianity can be seen in its three branches: Catholicism, Protestantism, and Orthodoxy. Catholicism's interest in ecology is illustrated in Pope John Paul II's encyclical of 1990: *The Ecological Crisis: A Common Responsibility.* The pope made several comments relevant to species preservation: "Ecological balances are upset by the uncontrolled destruction of animal and plant life or by a reckless exploitation of material resources. . . . The cosmos is endowed with its own integrity, its own internal dynamic balance."[17] The last statement seems remarkably harmonious with the Gaia hypothesis—the controversial scientific theory that claims that the universe is one large organism.

Closer to home, the United States Catholic Conference has prepared and sent to each parish an appealing packet titled "Peace with God the Creator, Peace with all Creation." This material naturally emphasizes the pope's encyclical, refers to the dynamic interrelationship that all creatures share with one another, and calls for respect for all creatures.[18] Furthermore, American Catholic theologians and ethicists now highlight caring for creation, including Rosemary Radford Ruether, an ecofeminist Catholic theologian who has written *Gaia and God: An Ecofeminist Theology of Earth Healing.*[19]

American Protestants do not have one person or group to speak for them, but in a study of what American Protestant denominations are saying I discovered serious concern about the environmental situation in general and about biodiversity in particular. A limited sampling includes the following:

[Christian] responsibility for a habitable planet is not just for human life, but for all creation.

—American Baptist

[Christians have a responsibility to] promote a more ecologically just world and a better quality of life for all creation.

—United Methodist

[God's covenant with Noah was with every living creature (Gen. 9:12), for] the individual of every species is dependent on the healthy functioning of its community, and human community depends on the vitality and stability of the biotic community.

—Presbyterian Church (U.S.A.)

Humans were created for mutually sustaining relationships with one another, with the rest of creation and with God.

—Church of the Brethren

The loss of genetic resources as animal and plant habitats are being destroyed is a big problem.

—Mennonite Church

[We are] called to acknowledge our interdependence with other creatures and to act locally and globally on behalf of all creation.

—Evangelical Lutheran Church of America

We need to strengthen and deepen our spiritual unity with nature.

—Friends Committee on Unity

It appears that interest in environmental issues within Protestant denominations is considerable. A representative of the evangelical wing of Protestantism has even declared that ecology is the ultimate pro-life issue.[20] And Sally McFague, a Protestant ecofeminist theologian, has written an insightful book on *The Body of God: An Ecological Theology*.[21]

Within the Orthodox branch of Christianity the view of panentheism has been consistently espoused. Russian Orthodox monks maintain close relations with nature, and the Russian Orthodox writer Dostoyevsky spoke of loving everything in all creation. It has been said that the Greek Orthodox Church in America has expanded its definition of sin to include sins against nature, such as forcing a species into extinction.[22]

Christian ideas about ecology have also materialized in ecumenical groups such as the National Council of Churches in the United States and the World Council of Churches. A packet on ecology produced by the National Council, called *God's Earth Our Home*, makes the point that birds, mammals, reptiles, fish, shellfish, insects, and so on, are living beings. Our lives would be poorer without these creatures. The packet contains an excellent article by John D. Paarlberg, "Protecting the Diversity of Life," which deals with the importance of biodiversity and things that can be done to support preservation of species.[23] The World Council of Churches has a working group devoted to "Justice, Peace, and the Integrity of Creation." The phrase "integrity of creation" implies the value of all creatures in and for themselves, for one another, and for God, as well as their interconnectedness in a diverse whole that has unique value for God.[24]

Islam

Islam shares many beliefs with Judaism and Christianity, including belief in a creator God. Muslims also believe that God is in the things God has made; a sacramental view of the universe is present in Islam. The Qur'an states that "assuredly the creation of the heavens and earth is greater than the creation of humankind, yet most people understand not."[25] Thus, all creatures are worthy of respect; humans should preserve, protect, and promote their fellow creatures. Humans are supposed to be maintainers, not owners.

A Sufi scholar originally trained in science, Dr. Seyyed Hosein Nasr, has written many books about Islam. In commenting on "Islam and the Environmental Crisis," Nasr argues that in Islam there is no clear separation between the natural and human worlds; the Qur'an actually addresses both. In Islam, nature contains signs of an all-encompassing God, who can be seen everywhere. All created things proclaim God's praise. Nasr contends that St. Francis's approach to nature is similar to that of Muslims. Also, the Islamic religion regards humans as the vicegerents of God, responsible for caring for God's creation. A gerent is one who rules or manages; the etymology suggests bearing or carrying. The idea of manager shows affinities with the idea of stewardship, but the role of vicegerent implies close relationship with God. The sense of working with God enables humans to go beyond anthropocentrism.[26]

Hinduism

A basic belief of Hindus is that Brahman, ultimate reality, is the source of everything that exists. All beings and creatures are related to Brahman and thus to one another. Hindus are reluctant to injure other creatures (the teaching of ahimsa). Members of the Jain sect actually refuse to kill anything, even insects. The Hindu teachings of karma and reincarnation also engender nonviolence, for animals may contain the souls of those humans not yet liberated. Reincarnation thus leads to reverence for other species. Humans have no special privilege or authority over other creatures. Some

Hindus claim that because of British colonialism Hindu beliefs were suppressed, and that under Western influence the people of India became materialistic. Further, Hindus also argue that the caste system benefited the environment because it reduced competition. And the Chipko tree-hugging activity of recent times has antecedents in a fifteenth-century movement. By "awakening the spirit of Hinduism," O. P. Dwivedi believes that Hindus can make a wholesome contribution toward alleviating environmental degradation.[27]

Buddhism

The Buddhist religion places great emphasis on everything being connected. Bhikku Buddhadosa said, "Nothing exists independently; everything exists interdependently."[28] A good Buddhist does not seek first his own entrance into nirvana, but the entrance of all living creatures. A Buddhist does not seek mastery over others, but mastery over self. Thich Nhat Hanh, a Vietnamese Buddhist monk, has written about walking meditation, in which one puts down each foot in mindfulness that one is walking on the wondrous earth.[29] Buddhists seek to promote compassion for all life; they do not kill animals or cut down trees. The Dalai Lama, who preaches peaceful living with all, including nature, exemplifies Buddhism's ecological ideals.

Taoism

This Chinese religion also views the world as an interconnected organic whole, in which every particular thing exists as a manifestation of the Tao (ultimate reality). Everything should live in harmony with others and with the Tao. A verse from the *Tao-te Ching* captures the essence of Taoism's view of the natural world: "The gentle way (Tao) of the universe has no form, yet it unites all tangles. It has no glare, yet it merges all light. It harmonizes all things and unites them as one integral whole."[30] Many Westerners regard Taoism as a model ecological religion.

Native American Religions

In addition to the major world religions, there are a host of more localized religions often called primitive or indigenous religions. The religions of the Native Americans (or American Indians) are part of this category. The ecological themes of Native American religions are appealing. David Kinsley points to three strong themes: hunting as a sacred occupation, rapport with animals, and rapport with the land.[31] Native Americans learned how to live with nature: they did not destroy, pollute, or use up. When Europeans came to the Americas they called the land a wilderness because it was so unspoiled. Native Americans believe that spiritual beings dwell in plants and animals. They thus regard themselves as relatives to animals, not as superiors. They see nature as alive, and look on the earth and its surroundings as beautiful. Native Americans believe that a sacred power pervades all natural forms. Long before the science of ecology emerged, Native Americans saw things as related. The words attributed to Chief Seattle capture the ecological attitude of Native Americans: "Every part of this soil is sacred in the estimation of my people. Every hillside, every valley, every plain and grove, has been hallowed by some sad or happy event in days long vanished. Even the rocks, which seem to be dumb and dead as they swelter in the sun along the silent shore, thrill with memories of stirring events connected with the lives of my people."[32]

Interreligious Dialogue

Beyond the particular religions mentioned, a dialogue between world religions has emerged. This dialogue achieved a significant boost in the September 1993 meeting of the Parliament of the World's Religions in Chicago. The *Declaration* of this gathering speaks often of caring for the earth. The following sentences are representative: "A human person is infinitely precious and must be unconditionally protected. But likewise the lives of animals and plants which inhabit this planet with us deserve protection, preservation and care. Limitless exploitation of the natural foundations of life, ruthless destruction of the biosphere, and militarization of the cosmos are all outrages. As human beings we have a special responsibility—especially with a view to future generations—for earth and the cosmos, for the air, water and soil. We are all intertwined together in this cosmos and we are all dependent on each other. Therefore the dominance of humanity over nature and the cosmos must not be encouraged. Instead we must cultivate living in harmony with nature and the cosmos."[33] Other examples of interreligious dialogue on this and other issues exist; they demonstrate that religious communities are seriously tackling the great moral issues of our day.

Religion and Science

The close relation between environmental ethicists and scientists has been noted. It can also be mentioned that in May 1992 a group of religious leaders and scientists came together in Washington D.C. to discuss the environmental crisis and what to do about it. This group subsequently issued "A Joint Appeal by Religion and Science for the Environment." This Appeal deals with the pressing issues of the environmental crisis and says, among many things, that "we are causing the extinction of species at a pace not seen since the age of the dinosaurs." The Appeal further declares, "We believe that science and religion, working together, have an essential contribution to make toward any significant mitigation and resolution of the environmental crisis." The Appeal pledges, again among many different things, a commitment to "slow the decline of species diversity."[34]

Dialogue and Cooperation

When I undertook the study of this issue, I was not sure if religious and philosophical ethics would have much in common on the issue of species preservation. If my observations are correct, however, there is definitely a lot of agreement. And the things agreed on are significant.

First, both philosophical and religious ethics seem to be very comfortable in the ways they utilize science. Both seem to realize how difficult it would be to adequately describe the species problem without the help of scientific research and knowledge. Both are open to science and, in the process, both have learned much from it.

Second, both philosophical and religious ethics acknowledge the deep necessity of going beyond anthropocentrism—making humans and their valuings the only important concern. Of course, humans will always matter, a great deal. But the nonhuman world also matters a lot. The natural world of animals and plants, and the ecological matrix that supports them, are enormously valuable, in themselves and for humans.

Third, both philosophical and religious ethicists wrestle with the moral concepts of good and right. In regard to species loss, utilitarian ethicists focus on doing as much good as possible for all sentient beings. Deontological ethicists place the emphasis on our duty to endangered species, on doing what is right. The concepts of good and right are also demonstrated in what religious ethicists say about biodiversity.

Perhaps most impressive is the agreement between religious leaders and scientists on both the problems and the possible solutions to the environmental crisis. I think the consensus reached between these groups in May 1992 was remarkable, and I wonder why the media paid so little attention to this event. These people are very different—in background, experiences, ways of thinking, and so forth. Their worldviews (metaphysics and views of reality) are probably incommensurable and incompatible. In spite of these differences they came to similar goals: taking better care of the natural world and embracing the biodiversity that is so eminently desirable.

Religion and morality can be relational. Religious and philosophical ethics can converse and cooperate. For these possibilities, we should indeed be grateful!

Notes

Chapter 1.
What is Religion?

1. These words are used frequently by scholars who refer to the different aspects or dimensions of religion.

2. Ninian Smart, *Worldviews: Crosscultural Explorations of Human Beliefs* (New York: Charles Scribner's Sons, 1983).

3. These descriptions come from various sources, such as Robert Bellah, Hans Küng, Shakespeare, Jack Bemporod, Alvin Plantinga, James B. Pratt, Friedrich Schleiermacher, Sigmund Freud, Alfred Wallace, Jonathan Edwards, Richard Muow, William Tremmel, and Denise and John Carmody.

4. These descriptions come from Leonard Swidler, James Christian, David Wisdo, and Gordon Kaufman.

5. Walter Wink, *Engaging the Powers: Discernment and Resistance in a World of Domination* (Minneapolis: Fortress Press, 1992), 6.

6. These descriptions come from Clifford Geertz, William James, Paul Tillich, Peter Berger, Carl Jung, Jeffrey Reiman, Maurice Friedman, Julian Huxley, Huston Smith, and Robert Capon.

7. These descriptions come from Kitaro Nishida, John Hick, Clifford Geertz, Robert Nozick, Robert Capon, Max Müller, and Leonard Sweet.

8. Iris Murdoch, *Metaphysics as a Guide to Morals* (New York: Penguin Books, 1992), 426.

9. These descriptions come from Robert Van Wyk, Kenneth Cauthen, Cornel West, Edgar Brightman, and John Dewey.

10. These descriptions come from John Hick, Leonard Swidler, Richard Creel, William Tremmel, Max Müller, Edgar Brightman, Tu-Wei-Ming.

11. Wolfhart Pannenberg, *Ethics* (Philadelphia: Westminster Press, 1981), 59.

12. Harold Kushner, *Who Needs God?* (New York: Summit Press, 1989), 194.

Chapter 2.
What is Morality (from a Religious Perspective)?

1. Peter L. Singer, ed., *A Companion to Ethics* (Oxford: Basil Blackwell Publisher, 1991), x.

2. *The World Almanac and Book of Facts, 1994* (Mahwah, N.J.: Funk and Wagnalls, 1994), 33.

3. John Hick, *An Interpretation of Religion:Human Response to the Transcendent* (New Haven, Conn.: Yale University Press, 1989).

4. Denise Carmody and John Carmody, *How to Live Well: Ethics in the World's Religions* (Belmont, Calif.: Wadsworth Publishing Co., 1986).

5. The debate between Wogaman and Hauerwas is described in James M. Childress, *Faith, Formation and Decision* (Minneapolis: Fortress Press, 1992).

6. Sissela Bok, in Bill Moyers, *A World of Ideas* (New York: Doubleday, 1990), 1:245.

7. Hans Küng and Karl-Josef Kuschel, *A Global Ethic: The Declaration of the Parliament of the World's Religions* (New York: Continuum, 1993).

Chapter 3.
What Is Morality (from a Philosophical Perspective)?

1. Michael Landmann, *Philosophical Anthropology* (Philadelphia: Westminster Press, 1974), 48.

2. Robert Maynard Hutchins, ed., *Aristotle II*, Great Books of the Western World (Chicago: Encyclopaedia Brittanica, 1952), 348, 352.

3. Mortimer J. Adler, *Desires Right and Wrong: The Ethics of Enough* (New York, Macmillan Publishing Co., 1991).

4. David Little, "Ethics: Types and Theories," *Abingdon Dictionary of Living Religions,* ed. Keith Crim (Nashville: Abingdon Press, 1981), 240–242.

5. Immanuel Kant, *Fundamental Principles of the Metaphysics of Morals,* trans. Thomas K. Abbott (Chicago: Encyclopaedia Brittanica, 1952), 256, 268, 272.

6. Immanuel Kant, *The Critique of Practical Reason,* trans. Thomas K. Abbott (Chicago: Encyclopaedia Brittanica, 1952), 345.

7. Hans Jonas, *The Imperative of Responsibility: In Search of an Ethic for a Technological Age* (New York: United Church Press, 1985).

8. Wolfhart Pannenberg, *Ethics* (Philadelphia: Westminster Press, 1981), 59.

9. Basil Mitchell, *Morality: Religious and Secular* (Oxford: Clarendon Press, 1980), 129.

10. John Stuart Mill, *Utilitarianism* (Chicago: Encyclopaedia Brittanica, 1952), 448–450, 463.

11. Ibid.

12. Carol Gilligan, "In a Different Voice: Women's Conceptions of Self and of Morality;" *Harvard Educational Review*, 1977(47):481–517.

13. Baier, Annette C., "What Do We Want in a Moral Theory?" in Samuel Enoch Stump, ed., *Elements of Philosophy* (New York: McGraw-Hill Book Co., 1993), 120–126.

14. Sidney Callahan, *In Good Conscience: Reason and Emotion in Moral Decision-Making* (San Francisco: HarperSanFrancisco, 1991), 5 ff.

15. Jean-Paul Sartre, *Essays in Existentialism* (Secaucus, N.J.: Citadel Press, 1965), 43.

16. Iris Murdoch, "The Sovereignty of the Good," in Donald M. Messer, *A

Conspiracy of Goodness: Contemporary Images of Christian Mission (Nashville, Abingdon Press, 1992).

17. Jeffrey Blustein, *Care and Commitment: Taking a Personal Point of View* (New York: Oxford University Press, 1991), 5.

18. Werner Marx, *Toward a Phenomenological Ethics: Ethos and the Life World* (Albany, N.Y.: State University of New York, 1992), 32.

19. John Rawls, *A Theory of Justice* (Cambridge, Mass.: Harvard University Press, 1971), 11.

20. W. D. Ross, "The Right and the Good," in Tom L. Beauchamp, *Philsosphical Ethics: An Introduction to Moral Philosophy,* ed. Kaye Pace (New York: McGraw-Hill Book Co., 1982), 112.

21. Leonard Peikoff, *Objectivism: The Philosophy of Ayn Rand* (New York: E. P. Dutton, 1991), 214.

22. John B. Cobb Jr., *Matters of Life and Death* (Louisville, Ky.: Westminster/ John Knox Press, 1991).

23. Robert Nozick, *Anarchy, State and Utopia* (New York: Basic Books, 1974).

24. Daniel Callahan, in Robert Van Wyk, *Introduction to Ethics* (New York: St. Martin's Press, 1950), 5.

25. Owen Flanagan, *Varieties of Moral Personality* (Cambridge, Mass: Harvard University Press, 1993).

26. Ernest Wallwuk, *Psychoanalysis and Ethics* (New Haven, Conn.: Yale University Press, 1991).

27. Landmann, *Philosophical Anthropology,* 24.

28. Mary Midgley, *Can't We Make Moral Judgments?* (New York: St. Martin's Press, 1991), 162.

29. Landmann, *Philosophical Anthropology,* 24.

30. Iris Murdoch, *Metaphysics as a Guide to Morals* (New York: Penguin Books, 1992), 26, 55, 293.

31. This summary comes essentially from Beauchamp, *Philosophical Ethics,* 336–376.

32. James Q. Wilson, *The Moral Sense* (New York: Free Press, 1993).

33. From David Gautier, *Morals by Agreement* (New York: Oxford, 1987); Bernard Gert, *Morality: A New Interpretation of the Moral Rules* (New York: Oxford, 1988); David Brink, *Moral Realism and the Foundation of Ethics* (New York: Cambridge University Press, 1989); William H. Shaw, *Social and Personal Ethics* (Belmont, California: Wadsworth, 1993).

34. A. Phillips Griffiths, "Ultimate Moral Principles: Their Justification," *Encyclopedia of Philosophy,* vols. 7 and 8 (New York: Macmillan Co., 1967), 177–182.

35. William Frankena, *Ethics,* 2d ed. (Englewood Cliffs, N.J.: Prentice-Hall, 1993), 115–16.

36. Michael J. Perry, *Morality, Politics and Law* (New York: Oxford University Press, 1988), 15.

37. Anthony C. Cortese, *Ethnic Ethics: The Reconstruction of a Moral Theory* (Albany, N.Y.: State University of New York Press, 1993).

38. Martha C. Nussbaum, *Love's Knowledge: Essays on Philosophy and Literature* (New York: Oxford University Press, 1990), 5.

39. Edward Long Jr., *A Survey of Recent Christian Ethics* (New York: Oxford University Press, 1982), 16.

40. John Roth, in an editorial by James Wall, *Christian Century*, April 15, 1992.

41. James W. Fowler, *Weaving the New Creation: Stages of Faith and the Public Church* (San Francisco: HarperSanFrancisco, 1991).

42. Charles Scrivener, *The Transformation of Culture: Christian Social Ethics after H. Richard Niebuhr* (Scottdale, Pa.: Herald Press, 1988), 132.

43. Franklin I. Gamwell, *The Divine Good: Modern Moral Theory and the Necessity of God* (San Francisco: HarperSanFrancisco, 1990), 8.

44. D. Z. Phillips, *Through a Darkening Glass* (Notre Dame, Ind.: University of Notre Dame, 1982), 10.

45. James D. Hunter, *Culture Wars: The Struggle to Define America* (New York: Basic Books, 1991), 42.

46. William Frankena, *Thinking about Morality* (Ann Arbor: University of Michigan Press, 1980), 5.

47. Robert Louden, *Morality and Moral Theory* (New York: Oxford University Press, 1992), 6.

48. E. O. Wilson, in *The Biology of Morality: A Multidisciplinary Dialogue* (St. Paul, Minn.: Bethel College Press, 1992).

49. Van Rensselaer Potter, "Global Bioethics: The Science of Survival," *Insights in Global Ethics* 3, no. 1 (January 1993): 6–8.

50. John R. Searle, *The Rediscovery of the Mind* (Cambridge, Mass.: MIT Press, 1992).

51. Robert Wuthnow, *The Search for America's Soul: Evangelicals, Liberals and Secularism* (Grand Rapids: Wm. B. Eerdman's Publishing Co., 1989), 190.

52. Robert M. Pirsig, *Lila: An Inquiry into Morals* (New York: Bantam Books, 1991), 277.

53. Daniel Callahan and H. Tristram Engelhardt Jr., eds., *The Roots of Ethics: Science, Religion and Values* (New York: Plenum Publishing Corp., 1981), 437.

54. Louden, *Mortality and Moral Theory*.

55. Lawrence Kohlberg, *The Philosophy of Moral Development* (New York: Harper & Row, 1981), 1:406. "Just as stage 6 cannot answer the question 'Why be moral?', it also cannot answer the question of a commitment to moral education. To engage such questions is to enter the domain of ethical and religious philosophy, the domain of stage 7."

56. Perry, *Morality, Politics and Law*, 15.

57. Mortimer J. Adler, *Truth in Religion: The Plurality of Religions and the Unity of Truth* (New York: Macmillan, 1990), 113ff.

58. James Q. Wilson, *The Moral Sense*.

59. Gene Outka and John P. Reeder Jr., eds., *Prospects for a Common Morality* (Princeton, N.J.: Princeton University Press, 1993).

Chapter 4.
Religion and Morality Are Inseparable

1. Albert Friedlander, "The Geography of Theology," in *Dialogue with a Difference: The Manor Group Experience*, ed. Tony Bayfield and Marcus Braybrooke (London: SCM Press, 1992), 35.

2. Henry David Aiken, "God and Evil: A Study of Some Relationships between Faith and Morals," *Ethics: An International Journal of Social, Political and Legal Philosophy*, 68, no. 2 (January 1958): 85.

3. Mortimer J. Adler, *Truth in Religion: The Plurality of Religions and the Unity of Truth* (New York: Macmillan Publishing Co., 1990), 46.

4. Wolfhart Pannenberg, *Ethics* (Philadelphia: Westminster Press, 1981), 69.

5. John K. Simmons, *Beliefs and Believers*, PBS Television Course, 1991.

6. John F. Haught, *The Promise of Nature: Ecology and Cosmic Purpose* (Mahwah, N.J.: Paulist Press, 1993), 21.

7. William Frankena, *Ethics* (Englewood Cliffs, N.J.: Prentice-Hall, 1963), 85.

8. D. Z. Phillips, *Through a Darkening Glass* (Notre Dame, Ind.: University of Notre Dame, 1982).

9. Os Guiness, *The American Hour: A Time of Reckoning and the Once and Future Role of Faith* (New York: Free Press, 1993), 149.

10. Kent Greenawalt, *Religious Convictions and Political Choice* (New York: Oxford University Press, 1988), 145.

11. Stephen L. Carter, *The Culture of Disbelief: How American Law and Politics Trivialize Religious Devotion* (New York: Basic Books, 1993).

12. James F. Drane, *Religion and Ethics* (Ramsey, N.J.: Paulist/Newman Press, 1976), 31ff.

13. *Ibid.*, 63.

14. Kitaro Nishida, *An Inquiry into the Good*, trans. Masao Abe and Christopher Ives (New Haven, Conn.: Yale University Press, 1990), 152.

15. Ronald M. Green, *Religious Reason: The Rational and Moral Basis of Religious Belief* (New York: Oxford University Press, 1978).

16. Alvin Plantinga and George Mavrodes, in J. E. Barnhart, *Religion and the Challenge of Philosophy* (Totowa, N.J.: Littlefield, Adams & Co., 1980), 193.

17. Haught, *The Promise of Nature*, 21.

18. Louis P. Pojman, *Ethics: Discovering Right and Wrong* (Belmont, Calif.: Wadsworth Publishing Co., 1990), 193.

19. James M. Gustafson, *Theology and Christian Ethics* (Philadelphia: Pilgrim Press, 1974), 23.

20. Karen Armstrong, *A History of God* (New York: Alfred A. Knopf, 1993), 389.

21. Quoted in Hans Küng, *Global Responsibility: In Search of a New World Ethic* (New York: Crossroad, 1991), 34.

22. Larry D. Shinn, *Two Sacred Worlds* (Nashville: Abingdon Press, 1977), 199.

23. Quoted in Küng, *Global Responsibility*, 47.

24. Basil Mitchell, *Morality: Religious and Secular* (Oxford: Clarendon Press, 1980), 7.

25. Lewis Smedes, *Choices: Making Right Decisions in a Complex World* (San Francisco: HarperSanFrancisco, 1986), 121.

26. Paul Tillich, *Morality and Beyond* (New York: Harper & Row, 1963), 15, 17–30.

27. Franklin I. Gamwell, *The Divine Good: Modern Moral Theory and the Necessity of God* (San Francisco: HarperSanFrancisco, 1990), xiiff.

28. Quoted by James Wall, *Christian Century*, October 16, 1991, 923.

29. Bernard Gert, *Morality: A New Justification of the Moral Rules* (New York: Oxford University Press, 1988), 164.

Chapter 5.
Religion and Morality Are Separable

1. Ronald Green, "Morality and Religion," *Encyclopedia of Religion*, ed. Mircea Eliade (New York: Macmillan Publishing Co., 1987), 10:93.

2. Robin Gill, *Christian Ethics in Secular Worlds* (Edinburgh: T. & T. Clark, 1991), 100.

3. From Gene Outka and John P. Reeder Jr., eds., *Religion and Morality* (Garden City, N.Y.: Doubleday & Co., 1973), 18.

4. Edward Long Jr., *A Survey of Recent Christian Ethics* (New York: Oxford University Press, 1982), 145.

5. From Jaroslav Pelikan, *The World Treasury of Religious Thought* (Boston: Little, Brown & Co., 1990), 60.

6. Samuel P. Oliner and Pearl M. Oliner, *The Altruistic Personality: Rescuers of the Jews* (New York: Free Press, 1988), 174–75.

7. From Bill Moyers, *A World of Ideas* (New York: Doubleday, 1989), 1:272.

8. Mary Midgley, *Can't We Make Moral Judgments?* (New York: St. Martin's Press, 1991), 15.

9. Lewis Smedes, *Choices: Making Right Decisions in a Complex World* (San Francisco: HarperSanFrancisco, 1986), 95–99.

10. Outka and Reeder, eds., *Religion and Morality*, 10.

11. Diogenes Allen, *Christian Belief in a Postmodern World* (Louisville, Ky.: Westminster/John Knox Press, 1989), 123.

12. Robert McAfee Brown, *Persuade Us to Rejoice: The Liberating Power of Fiction* (Louisville, Ky.: Westminster/John Knox Press, 1992), 35–37.

13. John C. Merkle, *The Genesis of Faith: The Depth Theology of Abraham Joshua Heschel* (New York: Macmillan Publishing Co., 1985), 221.

14. Unsigned article in *Philosophy and Public Policy* 6 (College Park, Md.: University of Maryland), no. 2 (Spring 1986): 2.

15. Richard B. Brandt, *Ethical Theory: The Problems of Normative and Critical Ethics* (Englewood Cliffs, N.J.: Prentice-Hall, 1959), 71.

16. James F. Drane, *Religion and Ethics* (Ramsey, N.J.: Paulist/Newman Press, 1976), 56.

17. Bernard Gert, *Morality: A New Justification of the Moral Rules* (New York: Oxford University Press, 1988), 165.

18. Vincent McNamara, *Faith and Ethics* (Washington, D.C.: Georgetown University Press, 1985), 206.

19. Unsigned article, *Philosophy and Public Policy* 6, no. 2 (Spring 1986): 2.

20. Gilbert Meilander, *Faith and Faithfulness: Basic Themes in Christian Ethics* (Notre Dame, Ind.: University of Notre Dame, 1991).

21. Robert Van Wyk, *Introduction to Ethics* (New York: St. Martin's Press, 1990), 42–43.

22. Jacques Thiroux, *Ethics: Theory and Practice* (New York: Macmillan Publishing Co., 1986), 24.

23. Long, *A Survey of Recent Christian Ethics,* 190.

24. Published by American Humanist Association (Amherst, New York: Prometheus Press, 1973).

25. Mary Midgley, *Science as Salvation: A Modern Myth and Its Meaning* (New York: Routledge, Chapman & Hall, 1993).

26. Mary Midgley, *Can't We Make Moral Judgments?* 15.

27. James Q. Wilson, *The Moral Sense* (New York: Free Press, 1993).

28. Collected papers of a Bethel College Conference, *The Biology of Morality: A Multidisciplinary Dialogue* (St. Paul, Minn.: Bethel College Press, 1992).

29. Gene Outka and John P. Reeder Jr., eds., *Prospects for a Common Morality* (Princeton, N.J.: Princeton University Press, 1993), 10.

30. Os Guiness, *The American Hour: A Time of Reckoning and the Once and Future Role of Faith* (New York: Free Press, 1993), 149.

Chapter 6.
Religion and Morality Are Relational

1. Fritjof Capra and David Steindl-Rast, *Belonging to the Universe* (San Francisco: HarperSanFrancisco, 1991), x–xiii.

2. In John M. Templeton and Robert L. Hermann, *The God Who Would Be Known: Revelations of the Divine in Contemporary Science* (San Francisco: HarperSanFrancisco, 1989), 201.

3. John F. Haught, *The Promise of Nature: Ecology and Cosmic Purpose* (Mahwah, N.J.: Paulist Press, 1993), 126.

4. David K. Fraser and Anthony Campolo, *Sociology through the Eyes of Faith* (San Francisco: HarperSanFrancisco, 1992), xv.

5. Sally McFague, *The Body of God: An Ecological Theology* (Minneapolis: Fortress Press, 1993), 15, 28, 199. Cf. Brian Swimme and Thomas Berry, *The Universe Story: From the Primordial Flaring Forth to the Ecozoic Era* (San Francisco: HarperSanFrancisco, 1980).

6. Carolyn Merchant, *The Death of Nature: Women, Ecology and the Scientific Revolution* (New York: Harper & Row, 1980), 99–100.

7. Joseph H. Kupfer, *Autonomy and Social Interaction* (Albany, N.Y.: State University of New York Press, 1989).

8. Leonard Sweet, *Quantum Spirituality: A Post-Modern Apologetic* (Dayton, Ohio: Whaleprints, 1991), 119.

9. H. Richard Niebuhr, *The Responsible Self: An Essay in Christian Moral Philosophy* (San Francisco: HarperSanFrancisco, 1963).

10. Wayne A. Meeks, *The Origins of Christian Morality: The First Two Centuries* (New Haven, Conn.: Yale University Press, 1993), 102.

11. Stanley Hauerwas and Alasdair MacIntyre, eds., *Revisions: Changing Perspectives in Moral Philosophy* (Notre Dame, Ind.: University of Notre Dame, 1983), 38.

12. Os Guiness, *Dining with the Devil: The Mega-Church Movement Flirts with Modernity* (Grand Rapids: Baker Book House, 1993), 84–86.

13. Paul Tillich, *Systematic Theology* (Chicago: University of Chicago Press, 1963), 1:71–79.

14. George F. Thomas, *Christian Ethics and Moral Philosophy* (New York: Charles Scribner's Sons, 1955), 377.

15. Bernard Williams, *Ethics and the Limits of Philosophy* (Cambridge, Mass.: Harvard University Press, 1985).

16. Edith Hamilton, *The Greek Way* (New York: W.W. Norton and Co., 1930).

17. James Davidson Hunter, *Culture Wars: The Struggle to Define America* (New York: Basic Books, 1991), 325.

18. Thomas, *Christian Ethics and Moral Philosophy*, 392.

19. E. G. Clifford Geertz, *The Interpretation of Cultures* (New York: Basic Books, 1973).

20. Harold Best, *Music through the Eyes of Faith* (San Francisco: HarperSanFrancisco, 1993), 94.

21. Meeks, *The Origins of Christian Morality*, 216.

22. William Sloane Coffin, *A Passion for the Possible* (Louisville, Ky.: Westminster/John Knox Press, 1993).

23. From the novel *Jane Eyre,* by Charlotte Brontë.

24. Meeks, *The Origins of Christian Morality*, 11.

25. Michael Ruse, in Steve Olson, *Shaping the Future: Biology and Human Affairs* (Washington, D.C.: National Academy Press, 1989), 179.

26. Unsigned article, "Religion and Morality," *Philosophy and Public Policy* 6 (College Park, Md., University of Maryland), no. 2 (Spring 1986).

27. Donald W. Shriver, "The Religious Roots of Charitable Giving," *Christian Century,* April 10, 1991, 403–5.

28. Kitaro Nishida, *An Inquiry into the Good,* trans. Masao Abe and Christopher Ives (New Haven, Conn.: Yale University Press, 1990), 152.

29. Jack Bemporod, "Morality and Religion," in H. Tristram Engelhardt Jr. and Daniel Callahan, eds., *Knowledge, Value and Belief* (Briarcliff Manor, N.Y.: Hastings Center, 1990), 63.

30. Basil Mitchell, *Morality: Secular and Religious* (Oxford: Clarendon Press, 1980), 149.

31. Richard Tarnas, *The Passion of the Western Mind: Understanding the Ideas That Have Shaped Our World* (New York: Ballantine Books, 1991), 407.

32. Franklin I. Gamwell, *The Divine Good: Modern Moral Theory and the Necessity of God* (San Francisco: HarperSanFrancisco, 1990), 209.

33. Max L. Stackhouse, "Politics and Religion," in *Encyclopedia of Religion,* ed. Mircea Eliade (New York: Macmillan Publishing Co., 1987), 2:408–23.

34. Vaclav Havel, in *Christian Century,* June 17–24, 1992, 603.

35. William K. Frankena, *Thinking about Morality* (Ann Arbor: University of Michigan Press, 1980), 94.

36. Ruse, in Olson, *Shaping the Future.*

37. Richard Hare, in Gene Outka and John P. Reeder Jr., eds., *Religion and Morality* (Garden City, N.Y.: Doubleday & Co., 1973), 28.

38. Haught, *The Promise of Nature,* 21.

39. Mary Midgley, *Science as Salvation: A Modern Myth and Its Meaning* (London: Routledge, 1992).

40. Michael Polanyi, in Leslie Newbiegin, *Truth to Tell: The Gospel as Public Truth* (Grand Rapids: Wm. B. Eerdmans Publishing Co., 1992).

41. Mary Midgley, *Can't We Make Moral Judgments?* (New York: St. Martin's Press, 1991), 162.

42. Jürgen Habermas, in Walter Wink, *Engaging the Powers: Discernment and Resistance in a World of Domination* (Minneapolis: Fortress Press, 1992).

43. Mitchell, *Morality,* 146.

44. Tarnas, *The Passion of the Western Mind,* 407.

45. Iris Murdoch, *Metaphysics as a Guide to Morals* (New York: Penguin Books, 1992), passim.

46. Sarvepalli Radhakrishnan, quoted in Jaroslan Pelikan, ed., *The World Treasury of Modern Religious Thought* (Boston: Little-Brown, 1990), 490.

47. Hunter, *Culture Wars,* 122.

48. Robert P. George, ed., *Natural Law Theory: Contemporary Essays* (Oxford: Clarendon Press, 1992), 11.

49. Lawrence Kohlberg, *The Philosophy of Moral Development* (San Francisco: HarperSanFrancisco, 1981), 1:412.

50. James M. Gustafson, *Theology and Christian Ethics* (Philadelphia: Pilgrim Press, 1974), 11.

51. W.W. Bartley III, *Morality and Religion* (London: Macmillan & Co., 1971), 97.

52. Robert Veatch, in Robert P. George, ed., *Natural Law,* 33.

53. Daniel Callahan and H. Tristram Engelhardt Jr., eds., *The Roots of Ethics: Science, Religion and Values* (New York: Plenum Publishing Corp., 1981), 435.

54. Stephen Toulmin, "Nature and Nature's God," *Journal of Religious Ethics* 13, no. 1 (Spring 1985): 37–52, which is a study of Gustafson's ethics.

55. George, *Natural Law Theory,* 13–15.

56. Walker Percy, *Signposts in a Strange Land,* ed. Patrick Samway (New York: Farrar, Straus & Giroux, 1991), 379.

57. Os Guiness, *The American Hour: A Time of Reckoning and the Once and Future Role of Faith* (New York: Free Press, 1993), 98.

Chapter 7.
Preserving Species

1. Worldwatch Institute, *State of the World* (W.W. Norton, 1988), 101–17; and *State of the World* (1992), 9–26.

2. From *This Week in Germany* (New York: German Embassy), June 28, 1996, 6.

3. Edward O. Wilson, *The Diversity of Life* (New York: W. W. Norton & Co., 1992), 215, 311, 344, 351.

4. Thomas Berry and Brian Swimme, *The Universe Story: From the Primordial Flaring Forth to the Ecozoic Age* (New York: Harper & Row, 1980).

5. Ian Barbour, *Ethics in an Age of Technology,* Gifford Lectures (San Francisco: HarperSanFrancisco, 1993), 2:60.

6. Peter Singer, *The Expanding Circle: Ethics and Sociobiology* (New York: Farrar, Straus & Giroux, 1981), 170.

7. Joel Feinberg, ed., *Reason and Responsibility* (Belmont, Calif.: Wadsworth, 1985), 523.

8. Stephen Jay Gould, "The Golden Rule: A Proper Scale for our Environmental Crisis," in Louis J. Pojman, *Environmental Ethics: Readings in Theory and Application* (Boston: Jones & Bartlett Pubs., 1994), 164–68.

9. Holmes Rolston III, *Environmental Ethics: Duties to and Values in the Natural World* (Philadelphia: Temple University Press, 1988).

10. Kenneth Cauthen, *Process Ethics: A Constructive System* (Lewiston, N.Y.: Edwin Mellen Press, 1984), 73.

11. Roger Gottlieb, ed., *The Sacred Earth: Religion, Nature and the Environment* (New York: Routledge, Chapman & Hall, 1996), 47.

12. *Ibid.,* 93.

13. *Ibid.,* 84.

14. *Ibid.,* 87.

15. Lynn White's article, "The Historic Roots of Our Ecological Crisis," originally appeared in *Science,* March 10, 1967.

16. Gottlieb, *The Sacred Earth,* 46.

17. *Ibid.,* 232–33.

18. From materials received from the United States Catholic Conference, 1995 and 1996.

19. Rosemary Radford Ruether, *Gaia and God: An Ecofeminist Theology of Earth Healing* (San Francisco: HarperSanFrancisco, 1992).

20. From materials received from the Protestant denominations listed, and an article in *Sojourners,* November 1993, quoting Tony Campolo.

21. Sally McFague, *The Body of God: An Ecological Theology* (Minneapolis: Augsburg Press, 1993).

22. Source unknown.

23. From *God's Earth Our Home,* National Council of Churches, 1994.

24. Gottlieb, *The Sacred Earth,* 268.

25. *Ibid.,* 268.

26. Steven C. Rockefeller and John C. Elder, eds., *Spirit and Nature: Why the Environment Is a Religious Issue* (Boston: Beacon Press, 1992), 85–106.

27. Gottlieb, *The Sacred Earth,* 151–62.

28. James M. Gustafson, *A Sense of the Divine: The Natural Environment from a Theocentric Perspective* (Cleveland: Pilgrim Press, 1994), 4.

29. Thich Nhat Hanh, *The Miracle of Mindfulness: A Manual on Meditation* (Boston: Beacon Press, 1976).

30. Gottlieb, *The Sacred Earth,* 67–68.

31. David Kinsley, *Ecology and Religion: Ecological Spirituality in Cross Cultural Perspective* (Englewood Cliffs, N.J.: Prenctice-Hall, 1995), 42–50.

32. Gottlieb, *The Sacred Earth,* 131–44.

33. Hans Küng and Karl-Josef Kuschel, eds., *A Global Ethics: The Declaration of the Parliament of the World's Religions* (New York: Continuum, 1993), 26.

34. Gottlieb, *The Sacred Earth,* 640–42.

Subject Index

Promotes use of science, how
matter, life and mind
evolved, ecology as a
science, 99–100
Advocates going beyond
anthropocentrism, 100

Relation of Religion and Morality:
The idea of relationality, 70
Relational views of reality, uni-
verse, self, 70–72
Process philosophy, 71
Going beyond derivation and de-
pendency, 72
Going beyond inseparable and
separable, 74
Allows both faith and reason, 75–77
Common elements in religious and
philosophical ethics, 78
Critical openness to each other,
78–80
Views of reality important to both,
86–88
Natural Law as bridge between
religion and morality, 88–92
Fosters a common morality, 93–95

Religion:
Difficult to describe, 1–4
Morality, a dimension of religion,
3, 45
Parts of religion, 4–8
Strengths of world religions, 11
Descriptions of world religions,
11–15
Views of nature, world religions,

15–17
Religious faith can lead to morality,
44
Western religions favor close ties to
morality, 45
Religious beliefs shape behavior,
46
Provides grounding for morality,
48
Influences culture and society,
53
No automatic connection to moral-
ity, 58
Moral codes accepted by faith, 54
Is more than morality, 57
Accepts separation of religion and
morality, 64–65
Engages in moral reasoning, 65–
66
Has a positive role, 80–84
World religions and biodiversity,
103–8 (*See* religious ethics)
Inter-religious dialogue and biodi-
versity, 109
And science, 110

Religious Ethics:
Similarity of morality and ethics,
9–10
Relation to philosophical/secular
ethics, 10
Historical precedence, 10, 47
Disagreements and agreements
within religious ethics,
17–19
And biodiversity, 102–9

An877-mn
83